HOW TO KEEP SCORE IN BUSINESS WILL TEACH YOU:

—what accrual-method accounting is
—how your cash flow affects your profit and loss
—where to look for hidden costs and assets
—the pluses and minuses of write-downs and write-offs
—the "80-20 rule" in determining your company's strengths and weaknesses
—how to ask your accountant for what you want, and how to understand the information he gives you
—and all the other vital elements of accounting and financial analysis that every executive must master

ROBERT FOLLETT is President of Follett Publishing Company, Vice Chairman of Follett Corporation, and director of a number of companies. He has written this book for young managers in his own company and in other companies to share with them the experience he has gained, and to help them avoid the mistakes he has made, on the way to his present top executive position.

All About Business from MENTOR

HOW TO KEEP SCORE IN BUSINESS

ACCOUNTING AND FINANCIAL ANALYSIS FOR THE NON-ACCOUNTANT

BY ROBERT FOLLETT

A MENTOR BOOK

NEW AMERICAN LIBRARY

TIMES MIRROR

New York and Scarborough, Ontario

Library of Congress Catalog Card Number: 80-80068

This is an authorized reprint of a hardcover edition published
by Follett Publishing Company.

SIGNET, SIGNET CLASSICS, MENTOR, PLUME, MERIDIAN AND
NAL BOOKS are published in the United States
by The New American Library, Inc.,
1633 Broadway, New York, New York 10019,
in Canada by The New American Library of Canada Limited,
81 Mack Avenue, Scarborough, Ontario M1L 1M8.

First Mentor Printing, July, 1980

3 4 5 6 7 8 9

Contents

1. Introduction

THE PURPOSE of this book is to teach you the fundamentals of keeping score in business. You will learn the basic workings of the accounting system. When you are through, you will be able to read, understand, discuss, and use a balance sheet, an income statement, and other statements found in financial reports. You will know something about various tools for analyzing financial reports and investment opportunities. You will have a basic vocabulary of the important terms used in accounting. You will be able to talk with more confidence to accountants, auditors, financial analysts, budget directors, controllers, treasurers, bankers, brokers, and lots of other people who use accounting jargon.

This book will not make you an accountant. But it will help you to talk with accountants. This book will not teach you to keep the books for a company. But it will help you to understand the financial reports produced by bookkeepers and accountants.

This is a book for non-accountants. It was written by a non-accountant. This book aims to make you successful in business despite your lack of formal accounting education or experience.

To get the most out of this book you will need three things. You will need to have a paper and pencil beside you as you read. You will need to have an electronic calculator (or a good head for computation.) Any cheap, simple calculator that can add, subtract, multiply, and divide will do. If you don't have one, I strongly recommend that you get one. Finally, you will need to have some time to get the most out of this book.

This is not a long book. But it will repay close attention. Some of the concepts are confusing. Some of the computations are a bit complex. There is nothing here that a good high school student cannot understand and handle. But it will take time. The time spent will be repaid with a basic understanding of business accounting.

The name of this book is *How to Keep Score in Business*. In business, the score is kept in dollars. The system of accounting provides the rules for keeping score. Some people don't understand keeping score in football. They get mixed up about touchdowns, safeties, field goals, and points after. And when there is talk of number of sacks, percentage completions, and yards per carry, they go blank.

A lot of people don't understand keeping score in business. They get mixed up about profits, assets, cash flow, and return on investment. Discontinued cash flow, current ratio, and book value per share leave them blank. This book will fill in some of the blanks.

Knowing how to keep score in business is essential to moving up in management. That's why seminars on accounting and finance for non-financial managers are among the most popular. That's why courses on this topic are offered at hundreds of colleges and other education centers. That's why hundreds of other books have already been published on this topic.

However, most of the seminars, courses, and books suffer from one major problem.

They are put together by accountants.

Most accountants know too much to explain the business scorekeeping system to the non-accountant.

I am not an accountant. I started my business career in sales. Then I had a lot to do with product development. Now I am the president of a large company. Along the way I have had to learn about financial accounting the hard way. I have worked with accountants, auditors, bankers, treasurers, controllers. These experts have flimflammed me with accounting lingo I didn't understand. I've been made to look like a fool because somebody with an accounting degree uncovered my ignorance. I've made almost every dumb mistake that a manager with no financial or accounting background can make.

But over 25 years in business I finally learned something about the accounting system. Now I can keep score along with the best. I don't know everything. But I know enough to be a good manager who can use financial information.

If you study this book carefully I'll give you 25 years of hard knocks and dumb mistakes distilled into a relatively few pages. When you're finished studying this book you will be well on your way to mastery of an indispensable management skill. You will know the basic system for keeping score in business. You will understand the major elements of financial accounting.

Here is how the rest of the book is organized:

In the remainder of this chapter you will learn why this book is about keeping score. You will see that scores are not the same as dollars. This key concept will underlie much of the rest of the book.

Chapter 2 is a glossary of key financial terms. Here you will find definitions of the key words and phrases most used by accountants. These are practical definitions that will develop the essential vocabulary you need for communication. You will want to refer to this glossary often—as you use the rest of the book and later when you deal with accountants and financial reports.

Chapter 3 introduces you to the balance sheet. This is a statement of a company's financial position. It is a basic financial report. In this chapter you will invest in the Acme Widget Company.

Chapter 4 tells more about the balance sheet. It will give you insight into what is shown and what is not shown. You will learn some useful methods of analyzing balance sheet information. Some valuable information never appears on any financial report. This will be discussed in this chapter.

Chapter 5 finishes the presentation on the balance sheet. When you are finished with this chapter you will have completed the most difficult part of the book—difficult because it introduces you to many new concepts and ideas. These will make it much easier for you to handle the other chapters that follow. They will make it much easier to handle real-life experiences with financial reports.

We turn to the income statement in Chapter 6. This financial report summarizes a company's operations over a period of time. The bottom line of the income statement is the famous "bottom line." You will learn what income statements show and what they hide. Various ways of analyzing income statements will be introduced. A brief section will show the reconciliation between the income statement and the balance sheet—how they connect together.

In Chapter 7 we discuss return on investment. Several methods of computing return on investment will be presented. Return on investment is an excellent way to evaluate company performance or to analyze possible investments or acquisitions. You will learn how to use this tool.

The statement of changes in financial position is presented and analyzed in Chapter 8. Use of this statement will help you to see how funds flow into, through, and out of a company. It reveals some of the things that are not too clear on the balance sheet or income statement.

Chapter 9 will teach you one method of making a cash flow budget. This is an especially valuable management tool. With it you can plan ahead and avoid the embarrassment of running out of cash, even when sales look good.

Chapter 10 introduces a variety of other analysis ratios and tools. Some are valuable to managers, some to lenders, and others to investors. I will caution you about the limitations of these ratios and tools. No substitute has yet been devised for common sense.

What will you have learned when you have finished this book? Chapter 11 is the summary chapter. It briefly recaps all of the major ideas presented in the preceding ten chapters.

This book has no pinup pictures. But it does have a lot of figures. You will find many of them in the illustrations included within the chapters and in the Appendix. At the back of the book is a Table of Present Values. You will learn how to use this valuable analysis tool in Chapter 7. You will want to use it frequently thereafter. The book finally ends with an Index where you can quickly look up things as you work with financial reports and accountants.

Have fun! Number-crunching and massaging of figures can be an enjoyable pastime—even if you have had no formal training. This book should give you enough information so you can crunch and massage with anyone.

THE FIRST LESSON—SCORES ARE NOT REAL DOLLARS

Basically, accounting is simple. Lots of people are accountants who aren't as smart as you are. Of course, the Internal Revenue Service, the Financial Accounting Standards Board, the Securities and Exchange Commission, and other organizations have made a basically simple system more complicated. To be a good manager you only need to know the basics. Let's begin with the most basic of basics—the "bottom line."

When people talk about the bottom line they usually mean the last line of an income statement which is labeled "Net Profit After Taxes" or "Net Income." This is the amount of money a business has to spend. Right?

Wrong!

Dead wrong. The bottom line, net profit after taxes, is just a score. The business may have many more actual dollars to spend than the bottom line figure shows. Or it may have a lot fewer dollars to spend. The bottom line is a score. Don't confuse the score with real money. For a long time I did. This led to a lot of dumb mistakes.

Learn this lesson and learn it well. The numbers you see on financial reports are scores in the game of business. They usually do not represent real, spendable dollars. In the remainder of this book you will be shown why this is so. You will also see how to figure out how many real spendable dollars a business has or is likely to have in the future.

Let's carry this further. You get a sales report. It shows the number of dollars of sales. Can the money from these sales be spent? No! In most businesses, sales figures are scores. The actual money will not be available until later, when the customers pay their bills.

You get a purchasing report. It shows that so many dollars worth of goods have been purchased and put into stock. Does that mean those dollars are spent and gone? No! In most businesses this is a score. The actual dollars will not be paid to the suppliers of the goods until sometime later.

And so it goes with most financial reports. These reports show scores. Scores are not the same thing as real, spendable dollars.

THE ACCRUAL METHOD

It is time to turn to a diabolical accounting invention—the accrual method.

Individuals keep track of cash. In fact, the IRS directs individuals to keep track of their cash expenditures and cash revenues for tax purposes. This means you don't have any revenue until you have cash in hand (or could have it). Just because someone owes you the money doesn't mean you have any revenue.

The same thing goes for your personal expenditures. If you want to take a deduction for a medical expense on your tax return, you actually have to pay the bill with a check or currency. Just because you visited the doctor and he sent you a bill is not enough to get you a tax deduction. Cash has to change hands.

None of this is true in business. In business, we use the accrual method of accounting, not the cash method.

If you used the accrual method, you would record your revenue whenever it was first owed to you—not when it was paid. You would record your expenditure when you got the doctor's bill—not when you paid it.

In business, there are similar examples of the accrual method. A sales transaction is recorded when the company makes up an invoice for the sale. The dollars are recorded on the financial reports at that time, even though the customer may actually pay days or weeks or months later.

The same thing happens in reverse when a company buys something. As soon as the company gets the bill for the goods or services it is buying, the cost is recorded in the company's financial records. The dollars involved in the purchase will show on financial reports, even though the company may not pay out those dollars for 30 or 300 days.

These are examples of the workings of the accrual system. Transactions enter the financial records as soon as they take place—not when the cash involved with the transaction changes hands. It is quite possible for a company to report big profits and be broke—unable to come up with enough cash to buy a cup of coffee. Conversely, a company may show a loss on its financial reports, even though it put cash in the bank.

The accrual method of business accounting guarantees that financial reports show scores, not real spendable dollars.

BUT SCORES ARE IMPORTANT

Before we leave this, let me say a word of caution. Don't think that scores are unimportant because they don't represent real dollars. Jobs are lost, promotions are won, raises are given, companies bought and sold on the basis of financial scores. You want to have good scores in business—even if they don't reflect the true cash status. Good scores produce winners in business just as good scores produce winners in sports.

In the rest of this book you can learn some ways to improve your scores.

2. Glossary of Key Financial Accounting Terms

THE BIGGEST PROBLEM most people have with an unfamiliar area is the vocabulary. They feel uneasy because they don't know the jargon. Professionals overwhelm the amateurs with confusing words and phrases.

This chapter gives practical definitions of 127 terms used in financial accounting. If you have some grasp of these words and phrases you will be able to deal with financial accounting and with accountants.

In some respects this is the most important chapter. That's why it is in the front of the book, rather than in the back where glossaries are usually found. Being able to cope with these terms will make the rest of the book much easier. It will also make your dealings with financial people and their reports much easier.

Read through this chapter quickly. Then go through it again more carefully. As you go on to later chapters, come back to this glossary whenever you need to refresh your understanding. Use the glossary when you need to interpret memos, bulletins, articles, and presentations by accountants, financial analysts, bankers, and so on. If you have a good grasp of the jargon you will be amazed at how well you can hold your own in discussions. Knowing the accounting vocabulary is a major factor in management success.

GLOSSARY

account—a record of financial transactions. Usually account refers to a specific category or type of transaction, such as travel expense account, or purchase account.

accountant—a person who is usually trained to understand and maintain financial records. (See bookkeeper, C.P.A.)

accounting—a system for keeping score in business, using dollars. Sometimes the way people refer to an accounting department where the score is kept.

accounting period—the period of time over which profits are calculated. Normal accounting periods are months, quarters, and years (either calendar or fiscal).

accounts payable—amounts owed by a company for the goods or services it has purchased from outside suppliers. (See liabilities—current.)

accounts receivable—amounts owed to a company by its customers. (See assets—current.)

accrual basis, system, or method—an accounting system that records revenues and expenses at the time the transaction occurs, not at the time cash changes hands. If you buy a coat and charge it, the store records or accrues the sale when you walk out with the coat, not when you pay your bill. Cash basis accounting is used by individuals. Accrual basis accounting is used by most businesses.

accruals, accrued expenses—a current liability which is an expense incurred but not yet paid for. Salaries are a good example. Employees earn or accrue salaries each hour they work. When they are paid, the accrued expense of their earned salaries is eliminated.

aging—a process where accounts receivable are sorted out by age. A debt that is only a few days old is a lot better than one that has not been paid for a year. Aging often sorts accounts receivable into current (less than 30 days after the sale was made), 30 to 60 days old, 60 to 120 days old, and so on. Aging permits collection efforts to focus on accounts that are long overdue. Aging also helps determine the amounts that should be put into allowances or reserves for bad debts or doubtful accounts. In valuing a company, the accounts receivable should be aged. A preponderance of old accounts may indicate that the accounts receivable asset is worth much less than is shown on the books.

amortize—to charge a regular portion of an expenditure over a fixed period of time. For example, if something cost $100 and is to be amortized over ten years, the financial reports will show an expense of $10 per year for ten years. If the cost were not amortized, the entire $100 would show up as an expense in the year the expenditure was made. (See depreciation.)

appreciation—an increase in value. If a machine cost $1,000 last year and is now worth $1,200, it has appreciated in value by $200. (The opposite of depreciation.)

assets—things of value owned by a business. An asset may be a physical property, such as a building, or an object, such as a stock certificate, or it may be a right, such as the right to use a patented process.

Current assets are those assets that can be expected to turn into cash within a year or less. Current assets include cash, marketable securities, accounts receivable, and inventory.

Fixed assets cannot be quickly turned into cash without interfering with business operations. Fixed assets include land, buildings, machinery, equipment, furniture, and long-term investments.

Intangible assets are things such as patents, copyrights, trademarks, licenses, franchises, and other kinds of rights or things of value to a company, which are not physical objects. These assets may be the important ones a company owns. Often they are not shown on financial reports.

audit—a careful review of financial records to verify their accuracy.

auditor—a person who makes an audit.

average collection period—the number of days required to collect accounts receivable, on the average: Average Collection Period=Accounts Receivable÷Sales×365. Average collection periods differ from industry to industry. When a company's average collection period gets longer, this indicates a problem. Customers may be getting into financial difficulty. Collection efforts may be sagging. Product quality or service may have declined so that customers have many complaints that must be resolved before they will pay. Or perhaps more liberal credit terms have to be given in order to induce customers to buy a sagging product line. Average collection period over the past several years should always be computed when analyzing a company.

bad debts—amounts owed to a company that are not going to be paid. An account becomes a bad debt when it is recognized that it won't be paid. Sometimes, bad debts are written off when recognized. Sometimes, a reserve is set up to provide for possible bad debts. This is usually called reserve or allowance for bad debts, or reserve or allowance for doubtful accounts. The write-off of a bad debt is an expense. Any addition to the reserve or allowance is also an expense. When there is a reserve or allowance, recognition of an actual bad debt will not result in an expense, since it has already been allowed for in expenses. Unrecognized bad debts for which no allowance or reserve has been set up are an important factor to consider in evaluating a company's value.

balance sheet—a statement of the financial position of a company at a single, specific time (often at the close of business on the last day of the year). The balance sheet normally lists all assets on the left side or the top of the sheet. All liabilities and capital are listed on the right side or bottom of the sheet. The total of all the numbers on the left side or top must equal or balance the total of all the numbers on the right side or bottom. A balance sheet balances. It balances according to this equation: Assets= Liabilities+Capital.

bond—a written record of a debt payable more than a year in the future. It shows the amount of the debt, due date, and interest.

book—a record of financial transactions.

bookkeeper—the person who keeps the books, or maintains the records of financial transactions. A bookkeeper needs less education or training than an accountant. Bookkeepers record transactions according to rules established by accountants.

book value—total assets minus total liabilities. (see also net worth or equity.) Book value is also used to mean the value of an asset as recorded in the company's books or financial reports. Book value is often different than the true value. It may be more or less. The book value of a share of stock is the total book value of the company divided by the total number of shares of stock.

breakeven point—the amount of revenue from sales which exactly equals the amount of expense. Sales above the breakeven point will produce a profit. Sales below the breakeven point will produce a loss.

budget—a plan for financial performance. Usually shows projected or planned revenues and expenses.

business—a type of commercial or industrial activity such as the steel business or the grocery business. Or, as often used in this book, any enterprise engaged in making, buying, or selling goods or services. Can be an individual enterprise, a partnership, a corporation, or another form of organization. Also company or firm.

C.P.A.—Certified Public Accountant, an accountant who has passed a professional test and is certified as qualified to do accounting and auditing.

capital—money invested in a business by its owners. (see equity.) On the right side of the balance sheet. Capital also refers to the buildings, machinery, and other fixed assets used by a business. Thus a capital investment is an investment in a factory, machine, or other item with a long-term use. A capital budget is the financial plan for the acquisition of capital assets such as factories or machines.

capitalize—to capitalize means to record an expenditure on the balance sheet as an asset, to be amortized over the future. The opposite is to expense. For example, research expenditures can be capitalized or expensed. If they are expensed, they are charged against income when the expenditure occurs. If they are capitalized, the expenditure is charged against income over a period of time usually related to the life of the development or products created by the research.

cash—money available to spend now. Usually money in the company checking account.

cash flow—the amount of actual cash generated by business operations within a period of time. Cash flow differs from profits shown because the accrual method of accounting is used and because non-cash expenses are deducted from profits.

chart of accounts—a listing of all the accounts or categories into which business transactions will be classified and recorded. Each account on the chart usually has a number. Transactions are coded by this number and can then be recorded, stored, and collected by data processing equipment.

company—a business enterprise. Company most often refers to the legal entity. Business may be used as a synonym for company but may also have other meanings.

contingent liabilities—liabilities not recorded on a company's financial statements, but which might become due. If a company is being sued, it has a contingent liability that will become a real liability if the company loses the suit. When evaluating a company, look for contingent liabilities.

corporation—an organization chartered by a state. The owners of a corporation are liable to the corporation's creditors only to the extent of the owners' investment in the corporation. If you buy a share of stock for $25 and the corporation fails, you cannot lose more than the $25. This limitation of liability has made the corporation the dominant form of business organization. Limited liability has made it possible to sell stock to raise money for new ventures.

cost accounting—a system of accounting concerned with assigning a fair share of costs to each unit produced. Cost accounting is primarily used in manufacturing companies. When costs are assigned to units, it is possible to arrive at unit selling prices and profits per unit. Many factors affect cost accounting. Most are beyond the scope of this book. Cost accounting is made complex by costs such as the cost of factory electricity, machine depreciation, and plant supervision, that are difficult to assign to specific units. Many cost accounting systems are the concept of standard cost—the cost that is expected for a unit. Actual costs are compared with standard costs to determine a variance. The variance is analyzed to see if it is caused by changing costs, changing selling prices, more or less units against which fixed costs are allocated, and so on. Analysis of the variance from standard cost helps to suggest management changes. Get a book on cost accounting if your position requires a knowledge of this specialized field.

cost of sales, cost of goods sold—the expense or cost of all items sold during an accounting period. Each sale made has a cost of that sale or a cost of the goods sold. In businesses that sell a few items, the cost of each item can be charged as an expense or cost of sales when that item is sold. In businesses with a great many items flowing through, the cost of sales or cost of goods sold is often computed by this formula: Cost of Sales=Beginning Inventory+Purchases—Ending Inventory. Cost of sales is a concept that is both difficult and important. It will be treated in great detail in this book. Cost of sales is not only affected by the cost of the items sold, but also by inventory obsolescence, inventory shrinkage, and FIFO or LIFO. (See these entries in the Glossary.)

credit—an accounting entry on the right side of a balance sheet. Usually an increase in liabilities or capital or reduction in assets. The opposite is debit. Each credit has a balancing debit. Accountants talk about debits and credits. Others seldom use the terms. Of course, credit has several other meanings in business usage, as in "You must pay cash, your credit is no good." Or "We have credited your account with the refund."

debit—an accounting entry on the left side of the balance sheet. Usually an increase in assets or a reduction in liabilities or capital. The opposite is credit. Each debit has a balancing credit.

debt—something that is owed. (See liability.)

deferred charges—see prepaid expenses.

deferred income—a liability that comes about when a company is paid in advance for goods or services and is liable to provide the goods or services later. For example, when a magazine subscription is paid in advance, the magazine publisher has income, but he is also liable to provide the subscriber magazines for the life of the subscription. The amount in deferred income is reduced as the magazines (or other goods or services) are delivered. The worth of a business is reduced by the amount of goods or services it is obligated to provide in the future.

depreciation—an expense that is supposed to reflect the loss in value of a fixed asset. For example, if a machine will completely wear out after ten year's use, the cost of the machine is charged as an expense over the ten-year life rather than all at once when the machine is purchased. Straight-line depreciation would charge an equal amount each year. A machine costing $1,000 depreciated over ten years by the straight-line method would have $100 charged to expense each year for ten years. Accelerated depreciation charges more to expense in the early years, less in later years. Under one accelerated depreciation formula the first-year charge for the $1,000 machine might be $181.82, the fifth year charge $109.09, and the tenth year charge $18.18. The choice of depreciation periods and methods is regulated by the IRS.

discounted cash flow—a system for evaluating investment opportunities. The system discounts or reduces the value of future cash flow since cash received in the future is not as valuable as cash available now. (See present value.)

dividend—a payment made to stockholders by a corporation, usually cash. A dividend is a portion of the profits paid out to the owners. It is a return on their investment. Dividends are paid with after-tax dollars. They are not a deductible business expense (as loan interest is, for example).

division—a portion of a company, usually operating more or less as a separate entity. Legally, a division is part of the parent company. A subsidiary is a separate legal entity owned by the parent company.

double entry—a system of accounting supposedly devised by an Italian monk in late medieval times. The system requires that every accounting transaction be recorded twice—as a debit and as a credit.

earnings—net profit after taxes. (See profit.)
Earnings per share are the company's total earnings for the accounting period divided by the average number of shares of stock outstanding.

80-20 rule—a general rule of thumb in business that says that 20 percent of the items produce 80 percent of the action—20 percent of the product line generates 80 percent of the sales, 20 percent of the sales force produces 80 percent of the orders, 20 percent of the customers produce 80 percent of the complaints, and so on. Of course, this rule is not accurate, but it does reflect the often-proved truth: nothing is evenly distributed; there is concentration. In evaluating any business situation be sure you find out which small group produces the major share of the transactions you are concerned with. Looking at things with the 80-20 rule in mind will sharpen your perceptions greatly.

equity—the owners' share of a business. Can be computed by subtracting liabilities from assets. (See also capital, net worth.)

expenditure—an expenditure is made when something is acquired for a business—an asset is purchased, salaries are paid, and so on. An expenditure will affect the balance sheet. It will not necessarily show up on the income statement or affect the profits at the time the expenditure is made. However, all expenditures eventually show up as expenses, which do affect the income statement and profits. Most expenditures involve the exchange of cash for something. Expenses need not involve cash. (See expense.)

expense—an expenditure chargeable against revenue during an accounting period. An expense results in the reduction of an asset. All expenditures are not expenses. For example, a company spends money to buy a truck. It trades one asset—cash—to acquire another asset. An expenditure has been made but there is no expense recorded. As the truck is used and depreciates, an expense is incurred. This concept of expense is one reason why financial reports do not show numbers that represent spendable cash. (See expenditure.) The distinction between expenditure and expense is important in understanding accounting. Expenditures occur when money (or something else of value) changes hands. Expenses occur whenever the expenditure is recorded so as to affect a company's profits. This is often at a different time than the expenditure. The expense of salaries is recorded before the expenditure of money for salaries is made. The expense of a machine purchase is recorded after the expenditure of money for the machine is made.

expense—to expense (a verb) means to charge an expenditure against income when the expenditure is incurred. The opposite is to capitalize. Expenditures in areas such as research may be expensed or capitalized. (See capitalize.)

FIFI, LIFO—stands for "first in, first out" and "last in, first out." These are two methods of determining cost of sales. Think of the inventory as a stack of goods. Each time new inventory is purchased it goes on the top of the stack. The oldest inventory is on the bottom of the stack. When a sale is made an item can be taken from the top or from the bottom of the stack. Taking from the bottom is FIFO. Taking from the top is LIFO. If the item sold is the last one put into the inventory stack, its cost will be the latest cost. If the item sold is at the bottom of the stack, its cost will be the oldest cost. This is very important in times of rapid inflation or deflation. In inflation, the last item in the stack will cost much more than the first item. Under FIFO the cost will be lower than under LIFO. A lower cost means higher profit—and more taxes to be paid. In a period of deflation, just the opposite occurs. Unfortunately, IRS will not permit companies to switch back and forth between FIFO and LIFO.

fiscal year—an annual accounting period that does not begin on January 1 and end on December 31. The federal fiscal year runs from October 1 through September 30. Many other fiscal years run from July 1 through June 30. A company can choose its fiscal year.

fixed asset—see asset.

fixed cost—a cost or expense that does not change as sales volume changes (in the short run). Fixed costs normally include such items as rent, depreciation, interest, and any salaries unaffected by ups and downs in sales. Of course, fixed costs are only fixed for the short run. (Leases can be cancelled, executives fired.) Extreme shifts in sales volume cause many fixed costs to become unfixed. Fixed costs are a factor in determining breakeven. (See variable cost.)

general and administrative expenses, G&A—expenses not attributable to specific business areas such as manufacturing, purchasing, or sales. The president's salary, franchise taxes, executive office rent, the company switchboard are examples of expenses normally included in G & A.

goodwill—in accounting usage, goodwill is the difference between what a company pays when it buys the assets of another company and the book value of those assets. For example, Company A buys Company B for $1,000,000. Company B has assets with a book value of $800,000. Company A adds these assets to its books. It must also account for the extra $200,000 it paid. Company A does this by entering in its assets the item "Goodwill—$200,000." Sometimes there is real goodwill involved—a company's good reputation, the favor of its customers, and so on. Sometimes it is just an overpayment. Other assets are used up in the course of business or are depreciated. Goodwill just sits there. There are no tax write-offs of goodwill. Companies search hard for ways to minimize the amount of goodwill they purchase.

income—see profit.

income tax—a tax levied by federal, state, or local governments on a company's profits or income. The tax is usually a percentage of the profits before taxes. What is left after income taxes is net profits after taxes.

inflation—an increase in prices or reduction in the value of money that has a major effect on companies and their financial reports. Since assets are shown at original cost, they do not reflect inflated value or the inflated cost of replacing them. Inflation of selling prices can result in increased dollar sales with reduced unit sales, and possibly reduced market share. Sales must go up faster than inflation if a company is to move ahead. Inflation distorts all financial reports. It also results in extra taxes being paid on the inflated income—which drains away cash needed to pay for the higher costs. Inflation corrodes all business.

interest—a charge made or rent paid for the use of money. The interest rate is normally expressed as a percentage of the loan to be paid for one year's use of the money. Interest paid by a company is considered a non-operating expense. Interest is non-operating income when a company earns it, unless the company's principal business is lending money.

inventory—the supply or stock of goods and products that a company has for sale. A manufacturer normally has three kinds of inventory: raw materials waiting to be converted into goods, work in process, and finished goods ready for sale. Inventory is a current asset.

inventory obsolescence—that amount of inventory which is no longer salable. Inventory obsolescence comes about from having more inventory on hand than can be sold. The inventory may be obsolete—old-fashioned, out of style. Or competition may have killed sales. Or too many may have been manufactured or purchased. The true value of a company's inventory is seldom exactly what is shown on the balance sheet. Often there is unrecognizable inventory obsolescence.

inventory shrinkage—a reduction in the amount of inventory that is not easily explainable. The most common cause of shrinkage is probably theft. Other causes are loss, damage by water, insects, fire, or other causes.

inventory turnover—a ratio that indicates the amount of inventory a company has to have to support a given level of sales. The formula is: Inventory Turnover=Cost of Sales÷Average Inventory. Retail businesses have a high inventory turnover—5, 10, or more times a year. This means they can produce a lot of sales with a small investment in inventory. The turnover number by itself is not too significant. Comparisons with the turnover of similar companies or with the turnover in previous years are more meaningful. If turnover goes down when sales stay up, this may signal that some parts of inventory are becoming obsolete. (Typically, a small portion of any inventory generates a large portion of the sales. A few items turn over very rapidly while others languish. See 80-20 rule.)

invested capital—the total of a company's long-term debt and equity. (See return on investment.)

journal—a chronological record of business transactions. Journal entries are usually transferred to the ledger.

leasehold improvements—amounts spent for permanent improvements to rented facilities, such as new walls, and lighting. These are fixed assets depreciated over the life of the lease.

ledger—a record of business transactions kept by account.

liabilities—amounts owed by a company to others.
   Current liabilities are those amounts that are due within one year or less. Current liabilities usually include accounts payable, accruals such as salaries earned by employees but not yet paid to them, loans due to be paid in a year or less, taxes owed and not yet paid, and so on.
   Long-term liabilities normally include mortgages,

bonds, and long-term loans. That portion of a long-term liability due within a year is usually included in current liabilities (such as the payments due this year on a mortgage).

liquid—having lots of cash or assets easily converted to cash. Lenders are usually concerned about a company's liquidity.

long-term, long-run—these phrases always mean longer than one year. Sometimes they mean far enough in the future so that current conditions can be significantly changed (new product developed, new plant constructed, and so on).

loss—the opposite of profit. An excess of expenses over revenues. A loss does not necessarily represent a reduction in cash during the accounting period. But eventually, a loss will be reflected in a reduction in cash.

marginal cost, marginal revenue—marginal cost is the additional, extra cost incurred by adding one more item. For example, if a plant makes 1,000 widgets a day, what will be the additional cost to make the one thousand and first widget? This is the marginal cost. Marginal revenue is the additional revenue coming in from selling one more item. According to economic theory, maximum profit comes at the point where marginal revenue exactly equals marginal cost. In practice, this is hard to hit. These concepts are used to consider whether or not to increase volume.

market—market, a noun, means that group of customers to whom one sells or tries to sell products or services. To market, a verb, means to determine customer needs or wants, create products or services to fill the needs or wants, sell to customers, and then distribute the resulting orders. Marketing is a total function from identification to satisfaction of a customer need or want.

market share—a company's sales as a percentage of the total industry sales to a market. If the total sales of widgets is 10 million a year, and Acme Widget sells 1 million a year, its market share is 10 percent. A high market share is an opportunity to achieve high profits (unless the high market share comes from excessive price cutting, or excessive selling expense). Financial reports of companies would be more useful if they showed market share for principal areas of business.

mortgage—a long-term liability or debt that is secured by specific property. Buildings and machines are often mortgaged. Most other debt is guaranteed by the general reputation and credit of the borrower and not by pledging specific assets.

net worth—total assets minus total liabilities. Net worth is the owners equity, capital, or stock plus retained earnings. Several terms mean the same thing. Net worth is not necessarily the true value of a company.

obsolescence—a reduction in the value of an asset caused by technological change, competition, altered business conditions, style changes, and so on. Machines can become obsolete long before they wear out (buggy whip machines, for example). Inventory becomes obsolete too, as newer models appear or customer tastes change. Obsolescence is recognized by a write-off or write-down of the value of the asset. This write-off or write-down (reduction in value) is an expense of the business when it is made. Obsolescence can be a significant expense in high-fashion or high-technology businesses. A major problem in evaluating a business is determining how much obsolescence has not been recognized. Assets are often not as valuable as they appear on the books. Obsolescence is a major reason.

opportunity cost—a useful concept in evaluating alternatives. For instance, if you choose alternative A, you cannot choose B, C, or D. What is the cost or the loss in potential profits of not choosing B, C, or D? This cost or loss of potential profits is the opportunity cost of alternative A. In personal life you may buy an automobile instead of taking a European vacation. The opportunity cost of buying an automobile is the loss of the benefits of the vacation. Too often, we look at costs for similar items. We compare one automobile against another. Shall we buy a Ford or a Chevy? We ignore the other things we could buy or do if we didn't buy the automobile at all. We ignore the opportunity cost.

overhead—a cost that does not vary with the level of production or sales, and usually a cost not involved in production or sales. Rent is usually considered overhead. The chief executive's salary is typically overhead, too. Overhead costs are difficult to allocate or apportion to any specific unit of sales or production. Fixed costs include overhead but may also include costs involved with production or sales which do not vary with volume.

partnership—a business in which two or more partners (persons, other partnerships, or corporations) pool their resources and share the profits. The partners are liable for partnership debts to the full extent of their assets. (Owners of corporations are only liable to the extent of their equity.) A limited partnership is a special form in which some partners have their liability limited to the amount of their contribution to the partnership while the general partner has all its assets subject to claims by creditors.

post—to enter business transactions into a journal or ledger or other financial record.

prepaid expenses, deferred charges—assets already paid for, that are being used up or will expire. Insurance paid for in advance is a common example. The insurance protection is an asset. It is paid for in advance, will last for a period of time, and expires on a fixed date. Travel advances are another common example of prepaid expenses.

present value—a concept that compares the value of money available in the future with the value of money in hand today. The present value of money is compared with the future value. To illustrate: $100 in hand today is worth more than $100 to be available in five years. This is because the $100 in hand today can be invested and earn money. If it is invested in a 5 percent savings account, the $100 will grow to $127.63 in five years. Or to put it another way, $78.35 invested at 5 percent for five years will grow to $100. Thus the present value of $100 received five years in the future is $78.35. The concept of present value is used to analyze investment opportunities that have a future payoff. All of the investment and all of the return can be computed at present value to see if the percentage rate of return on the investment is acceptable. Present value is more extensively discussed in Chapter 7.

price-earnings (p/e) ratio—the market price of a share of stock divided by the earnings (profit) per share of the company. A company whose stock is selling at $48 a share and whose current earnings for the year are $6 per share has a price-earnings ratio of 8. (A p/e of 8 is a common figure.) In periods of great speculation p/e ratios of hot companies may go as high as 40, 50, 100 or more. $6 per share earnings would have a market price of $240, $300, $600, or more. In a depressed economy or for dull companies in static industries, p/e's may be 3 or 4. In periods of speculation, companies try many tricks to boost p/e ratios so that their highly valued stock can be used in acquisitions or be sold at a high price. Price-earnings ratio is a poor method of evaluating the real worth of a company.

productivity—the amount of output per unit of labor, capital, and so on. Increasing productivity is a critical function of management. How can each sales representative sell more? How can each machine produce more? How can each file clerk file more? How can each dollar invested in a company produce more profit? Measures of productivity are valuable additions to financial reports.

profit—the amount left over when expenses are subtracted from revenues.

Gross profit is the profit left when cost of sales is subtracted from sales. Gross profit is before any operating expenses are subtracted.

Operating profit is the profit from the primary operations of a business. It is sales or revenues minus cost of sales and minus operating expenses. Operating profit is before non-operating income and expense, and before income taxes.

Net profit before taxes is the operating profits minus non-operating expenses and plus non-operating income.

Net profit after taxes is the bottom line. It is the final profit after everything has been subtracted. Also called income, net income, or earnings. Net profit after taxes is not the same as cash flow and does not represent spendable dollars.

retained earnings—profits not distributed to stockholders as dividends. Retained earnings are the accumulation of a company's profits less any dividends paid out. Retained earnings are usually not cash. They are normally invested in the various assets of the company.

return—a basic component in measuring business performance. Return is variously defined but most often is net profit after taxes.

return on investment, ROI—a measure of the effectiveness and efficiency with which managers use the resources available to them in the business.

Return on equity, ROE—usually net profit after taxes divided by the owner's equity, translated into a percentage. A recent survey of public corporations showed average return on equity (year-end) to be about 12 percent.

Return on invested capital, ROIC—usually net profit after taxes plus interest paid on long-term debt divided by owner's equity plus long-term debt. The investment in this formula is both equity and long-term debt. The return is both profit and interest that is a return on the long-term debt investment. A recent survey showed average return on invested capital to be about 9 percent.

Return on assets used, ROAU—usually the operating profit divided by the assets used to produce the profit. This method of computing return on investment is typically used for divisions of a company that have no control over liabilities or use of cash. These things are handled by the parent corporation or headquarters.

Return on investment measures are extremely useful in evaluating company performance. But ROI can only be used to compare consistent entities—similar companies in the same industry, or the same company over a period of time. Different companies may have different historic ROIs. Different industries usually have different ROIs. The minimum acceptable return on investment must be greater than that which can be realized on a safer investment. If an investor can earn a return of 5 percent in government-insured savings or securities, he will certainly expect a manager to produce better than 5 percent if the investment is made in a business venture with more risk.

revenue—the amounts received by or due a company for the goods or services it provides to customers. Receipts are the cash amounts received. Revenues include receipts as well as amounts owed to the company for the sales of goods or services. (See sales.)

risk—the possibility of loss; inherent in all business activities. Related to return. Low risk will be satisfied with low return. High risk requires high return. Risk is difficult to measure, but all business decisions need to take into account the amount of risk involved.

rounding off—many accountants present financial reports that show numbers exact to the penny. This is unnecessary and often confuses analysis. As a manager, I have found that financial reports and budgets rounded off to the nearest thousand dollars are satisfactory.

sales—the amounts received or due a company for goods or services sold to customers. (See revenue.)

Gross sales are the total sales before any returns or adjustments.

Net sales are gross sales minus any returns or adjustments made during the accounting period. Sales usually do not include sales taxes or transportation. Unless it is a business that sells for cash, sales don't represent cash. Cash will come in later when the customer pays the bill. A company cannot live without sales.

short-run, short-term—a period of time too short to allow significant changes in operations. Usually defined as a year or less.

stock—a certificate that indicates ownership of a portion of a corporation. A share of stock.

Preferred stock promises its owner a dividend that is usually fixed in amount or percent. Preferred stockholders have preference. If there are any profits, they get paid first.

Common stock has no preference and no fixed rate of return. It is the most common kind of stock.

Treasury stock is stock originally issued to stockholders but returned to the corporation by purchase or as a gift.

Authorized but unissued stock—the number of shares of stock a company can have is usually set by its charter or by official corporate action. If a corporation is authorized to have one million shares and it sells 750,000, then it has 250,000 authorized but unissued shares. These may be sold later or used to acquire another company.

stocks of goods—refers to the inventory, stock on hand, available for sale. The stockroom is where inventory is kept. Overstocked means that too much inventory is on hand.

subsidiary—a company owned or controlled by another company. A subsidiary is a separate legal entity. A division is not.

sunk costs—money already spent and gone, which will not be recovered no matter what course of action is followed. In comparing alternate courses of action, it is usually wise to forget about sunk costs. Bad decisions are made when managers pretend they can somehow recoup sunk costs.

surplus—see retained earnings.

tax—an amount paid to a governmental body.

Income tax is a portion or percentage of the net profit before taxes.

Franchise tax is a tax paid on the right to do business. It may be a flat sum or related to something like the amount of original capital. It is not related to profits.

Property tax is a tax levied on the value of the property or assets of a company.

Sales tax is a tax collected by business as a percentage of the sales price and then sent to the taxing government. The business acts as the tax collector for the sales tax.

The kinds of taxes are many and limited only by the ingenuity of governmental bodies. Taxes have a major impact on business and business decisions. As a general principle: Don't make any decisions for tax reasons that would not be a good decision without tax considerations.

trial balance—at the close of an accounting period, the transactions posted in the ledger are added up—those which affect assets and those which affect liabilities and capital. A test or trial balance sheet is prepared with assets on one side and liabilities and capital on the other. The two sides should balance. If they don't, the accountants must search through the transactions to find the reason why. They must make the balance sheet balance.

variable cost—a cost that changes as sales or production change. If a business is producing nothing and selling nothing, the variable cost should be zero. Fixed costs will continue regardless of production or sales levels.

working capital—current assets minus current liabilities. In most businesses the major components of working capital are accounts receivable and inventory minus accounts payable. As a business grows it will have more accounts receivable and will need more inventory. Thus its need for working capital will increase. Increases in working capital can come from retained earnings, borrowing, or selling more stock.

write-down—the partial reduction in value of an asset, recognizing obsolescence or other losses in the value of the asset. (See obsolescence.)

write-off—the complete reduction in value of an asset, recognizing that the asset no longer has any value whatsoever.

3. The Balance Sheet

THE FIRST financial report we cover in this book is the balance sheet. The balance sheet shows the financial position of a business at one specific time. It is a snapshot of a business—not a record of its performance over a period of time. The balance sheet pinpoints financial status at the close of business at the end of an accounting period.

THE BALANCE SHEET BALANCES

The balance sheet has two sides. The numbers on each side must add up to the same total. The balance sheet balances.

On one side of the balance sheet are Assets (things of value the company owns). On the other side are Liabilities (debts the company owes) and Capital (the owners' share of the company). The balance sheet is described by this equation:

$$Assets = Liabilities + Capital$$

Every entry into or out of one part of the balance sheet must be balanced by a corresponding entry in another part of the balance sheet. This is so that the bottom totals will remain in balance. This is basic double-entry bookkeeping.

Words alone are not enough to convey the full meaning of all this. So we will construct a balance sheet of our own. Before we do that here are some illustrations of typical corporate balance sheets. If you have looked at any company financial reports you have probably already seen examples of balance sheets. Look at the illustrations. Do they follow the equation (Assets = Liabilities + Capital)? Do they balance?

29

balance sheet

ASSETS

	July 31	
	1977	1976
Cash	$ 75,986	$ 72,002
Accounts receivable (Notes A and C)		
Trade	64,998	99,502
Federal income tax	5,019	-0-
Other	19,776	-0-
	89,793	99,502
Inventory (Notes A and B)		
Materials and supplies	138,995	176,295
Work in process	33,978	23,155
	172,973	199,450
Prepaid expenses	8,176	5,639
Total current assets	346,928	376,593
Advance to affiliated company	-0-	70,180
Property, plant and equipment—at cost		
(Notes A and B)		
Land	56,460	56,460
Buildings and production lines	722,776	660,001
Shop machinery and equipment	175,090	157,774
Office furniture, fixtures and equipment	34,521	34,497
Autos and trucks	76,722	68,439
	1,065,569	977,171
Less accumulated depreciation	319,124	266,814
	746,445	710,357
Investment in common stock (Note F)	51,342	25,800
Other Assets	233	4,233
Total assets	$1,144,948	$1,187,163

LIABILITIES

	1977	1976
Current liabilities		
Accounts payable	$ 60,861	$ 22,803
Current maturities of long-term debt	53,939	41,218
Accrued liabilities		
Federal income tax	-0-	19,071
Other accruals	13,160	12,890
Other current liabilities	-0-	9,000
Total current liabilities	127,960	104,982
Long-term debt (Note B)	585,834	605,742
Less current maturities	53,939	41,218
	531,895	564,524
Total liabilities	659,855	669,506
Stockholders' equity (Note E)		
Common stock—1,000,000 shares of $1.00 par value authorized, 322,129 shares issued and outstanding in 1977; 10,000 shares of $100.00 par value authorized, 713 shares issued and outstanding in 1976	322,129	71,300
Additional paid-in capital	27,871	64,442
Retained earnings	135,093	381,915
Total stockholders' equity	485,093	517,657
Total liabilities and stockholders' equity	$1,144,948	1,187,163

The accompanying notes are an integral part of these financial statements.

HUNT MANUFACTURING CO. AND SUBSIDIARIES

Consolidated balance sheet

November 27, 1977 and November 28, 1976

Assets	1977	1976
Current assets:		
Cash	$ 392,831	$ 269,937
Accounts receivable, less allowance for doubtful accounts: 1977, $131,437; 1976, $120,034	6,373,722	5,430,935
Inventories:		
Finished and partly finished products	4,071,218	3,561,186
Raw materials and supplies	2,047,731	2,214,807
Prepaid expenses	187,253	84,842
Total current assets	13,072,755	11,561,707
Investment in affiliated foreign company	23,520	23,520
Property, plant and equipment, at cost, less accumulated depreciation	6,200,078	5,523,995
Intangible assets, at cost less amortization	661,982	711,420
Loans to officers, collateralized by cash value of life insurance	75,663	73,776
Other assets	68,369	85,458
	$20,102,367	$17,979,876

See accompanying notes to consolidated financial statements.

Liabilities & Stockholders' Equity

	1977	1976
Liabilities		
Current liabilities:		
Current portion of long-term debt	$ 418,987	$ 325,910
Accounts payable	1,210,152	1,156,933
Accrued expenses:		
Salaries, wages and commissions	1,060,291	802,416
Pensions	236,398	208,320
Income taxes	556,042	521,138
Other	544,199	497,394
Total current liabilities	4,026,069	3,512,111
Long-term debt, less current portion	2,223,566	2,726,530
Deferred income taxes	411,300	203,200
Stockholders' Equity		
Capital stock:		
Preferred, $.10 par value, authorized 1,000,000 shares; none issued	—	—
Common, $.10 par value, authorized 3,000,000 shares; issued: 1977—1,158,857 shares 1976—924,160 shares	115,886	92,416
Capital in excess of par value	273,305	264,342
Retained earnings	13,052,241	11,181,277
Total stockholders' equity	13,441,432	11,538,035
	$20,102,367	$17,979,876

See accompanying notes to consolidated financial statements.

Augat Inc. and Subsidiaries

Consolidated Balance Sheets, December 31, 1977 and 1976

Assets	1977	1976
Current Assets:		
Cash and time deposits..	$ 3,694,807	$ 1,230,112
Short-term investments — at cost which approximates market ...	300,000	350,000
Accounts receivable — less allowance for doubtful accounts, $252,636 in 1977 and $201,230 in 1976	9,769,190	7,456,090
Inventories:		
Finished goods	5,073,750	3,432,839
Work in process	1,528,863	1,173,327
Raw materials	5,193,265	4,320,238
Total inventories	11,795,878	8,926,404
Prepaid expenses	98,484	103,311
Total current assets	25,658,359	18,065,917
Property, Plant, and Equipment:		
Land	594,871	482,510
Building and building improvements	4,110,373	3,765,651
Machinery and equipment	12,801,878	10,701,102
Furniture and fixtures	806,569	687,709
Construction in progress	676,785	
Total	18,990,276	15,636,972
Less accumulated depreciation.................................	6,493,292	4,865,588
Property, plant, and equipment — net	12,496,984	10,771,384
Note Receivable	134,866	
....	570,750	415,489
otal..	$38,860,959	$29,252,790

See notes to financial statements.

WORKING CAPITAL
(In millions of dollars)

Augat Inc. and Subsidiaries

Consolidated Balance Sheets, December 31, 1977 and 1976

Liabilities and Shareholders' Equity

	1977	1976
Current Liabilities:		
Accounts payable		
Federal, state and foreign taxes payable	$ 2,810,643	$ 1,753,858
Current maturities of long-term debt	2,614,172	798,290
Accrued payroll and other compensation	59,900	59,700
Other accrued expenses	1,553,455	975,617
Total current liabilities	1,015,383	371,784
	8,053,553	3,959,249
Long-Term Debt	139,386	199,302
Deferred Income Taxes	1,176,887	982,887
Minority Interest	1,392,882	1,051,560
Shareholders' Equity:		
Common stock — authorized, 7,000,000 shares of $.10 par value; issued and outstanding, 3,578,913 shares		
Paid-in capital	357,891	357,891
Retained earnings	1,145,756	1,145,756
Shareholders' equity	26,594,604	21,556,145
Total	28,098,251	23,059,792
	$38,860,959	$29,252,790

See notes to financial statements.

SHAREHOLDERS' EQUITY
(In millions of dollars)

ACME WIDGET COMPANY

In order to construct our own balance sheet we need a company. Let's start one. We will call our company Acme Widget Company. We are going to buy a widget-making machine, purchase raw materials, and produce a whole lot of widgets. We will sell the widgets to widget users and make a lot of money—which we will share generously with the tax collector.

You and I are each going to put up $10,000. In exchange for this money we will get shares of stock in the Acme Widget Company. Figure 1 shows how this is recorded on the Acme Widget balance sheet.

Figure 1

ACME WIDGET COMPANY
Balance Sheet

ASSETS		LIABILITIES AND CAPITAL	
Cash	$20,000	LIABILITIES	$—0—
		CAPITAL	
		Common Stock	$20,000
	=====		=====
		Total Liabilities	
Total Assets	$20,000	and Capital	$20,000

On the asset side we record the $20,000 we put into the Acme Widget bank account as cash. On the liabilities and capital side we record the value of the stock certificates we were issued.

We need more money to get Acme Widget started. So we visit our friendly bank and borrow $15,000 for Acme Widget on a six-month loan. Figure 2 shows how our balance sheet looks after we get the loan.

In Figure 2 as in Figure 1, you can see that the transaction is recorded on both sides of the balance sheet and the bottom totals are the same. They balance.

Now we will buy a $12,000 widget-making machine. We will also buy $5,000 worth of raw materials to make widgets on the machine. We have gotten the machine and

Figure 2

ACME WIDGET COMPANY
Balance Sheet

ASSETS		LIABILITIES AND CAPITAL	
		LIABILITIES	
Cash	$35,000	Note Payable	$15,000
		CAPITAL	
		Common Stock	$20,000
Total Assets	$35,000	Total Liabilities and Capital	$35,000

the raw materials, but we have not yet paid for them. These bills will be due in thirty days.

We have also leased factory space. We paid a month's rent in advance—$250.

These transactions are recorded on the balance sheet as shown in Figure 3.

Figure 3

ACME WIDGET COMPANY
Balance Sheet

ASSETS		LIABILITIES AND CAPITAL	
		LIABILITIES	
Cash	$34,750	Accounts Payable	$17,000
Inventory	5,000	Note Payable	15,000
Prepaid Expenses	250	Total Liabilities	$32,000
Fixed Assets	12,000		
		CAPITAL	
		Common Stock	$20,000
Total Assets	$52,000	Total Liabilities and Capital	$52,000

Let's look at each item in Figure 3. Our cash is still all there, except for the $250 we paid in advance rent. We have acquired an inventory of raw materials—$5,000 worth. The rent is a prepaid expense (see Glossary) and is recorded at $250. The widget machine is a fixed asset. (Also see Glossary. As we use these various accounting terms, it is a good idea to go back to the Glossary to be sure you have an idea of what they mean.) We paid $12,-000 for the machine so that is its value as an asset at this time.

Now look at the liabilities. Accounts payable of $17,000 represents the $12,000 we owe to the widget machine supplier plus the $5,000 we owe to the raw materials supplier.

The note payable is the amount we borrowed from the bank.

Capital still shows our stock ownership of $20,000—our initial investment in Acme Widget.

Total assets are equal to the total liabilities and capital. The balance sheet continues to balance as we enter items in two places. For example, we put the value of the widget machine on the asset side and the amount we owed on it on the liability side. In the case of the rent payment, we added it to the assets as a prepaid expense but also subtracted it from our cash asset.

Each transaction during the course of the Acme Widget operations will be similarly recorded in two places so that the balance sheet always stays in balance. These transactions are usually not recorded directly onto the balance sheet. They go into journals (chronological records of transactions) and into ledgers (records of transactions by area or account, such as cash or accounts payable.) At the end of an accounting period the information recorded on the journals and ledgers is transferred to a balance sheet for the end of that period.

Accountants and other people use worksheets in preparing financial reports. It is time for you to learn how to prepare your own worksheet. Then you will go from that to the preparation of a balance sheet.

ACME WIDGET'S YEAR-END BALANCE SHEET

Acme Widget's operations during the year are going to affect a number of accounts. The balance sheet will need a number of headings to reflect the transactions. Listed below are the headings or accounts that you will be using on your worksheet.

ASSETS

Cash (cash available in the bank, or elsewhere, to spend.)

Accounts receivable (amounts owed to Acme by its customers.)

Inventory

    Raw materials (the stock of raw materials waiting to be made into widgets.)

    Finished goods (the stock of completed widgets ready to sell.)

Prepaid expenses (a payment made in advance. In this case, rent.)

Fixed assets (machinery, equipment, buildings, and so on, used over a long period of time in the business. In this case, the widget machine.)

Depreciation (the portion of the original cost of the fixed assets used up or expensed since purchase.)

LIABILITIES

Accounts payable (amounts owed by Acme to its suppliers.)

Notes payable (amounts owed by Acme to the bank or other lenders; due within a year or less.)

Accruals (salaries and taxes owed by Acme but not yet paid.)

CAPITAL

Common stock (the amount put in by investors to buy the common stock of Acme Widget Company.)

Retained earnings (the net profits after taxes of Acme Widget, less any dividends paid to stockholders. In terms of the worksheet you will see that items which do not affect other assets or liabilities do affect retained earnings by increasing or decreasing profits.)

If you need further help on these terms, go to the Glossary.

During its first year, Acme Widget has the following transactions:

1. Investors purchase $20,000 of common stock.

We saw this on the balance sheet in Figure 1. On a worksheet it might look like this:

1. $20,000 stock sale to Investors:
+ $20,000 cash / + $20,000 common stock

This worksheet entry shows that this transaction adds $20,000 to cash assets. It balances this by adding $20,000 to common stock capital. The slash separates the two balancing entries.

Take a piece of paper. 8½ X 11 will be fine. Put a label at the top. It should show that this is the worksheet for the Acme Widget balance sheet at the end of the first year.

After you have labeled your worksheet, put in entry 1 shown above. When you have finished, go on to entry 2 below. There will be 18 transactions given for Acme Widget's first year of operation. For the early ones, I will give you the entry I would put on the worksheet. For the later transactions you will make your own entries.

After you have completed your worksheet you will proceed to make up a balance sheet for Acme Widget Company. This kind of hands-on experience will be much more useful than just reading about balance sheets. So get your worksheet paper ready.

2. Acme borrows $15,000 from the bank on a six-month note or loan. (See Figure 2.) The worksheet might look like this:

2. Borrow $15,000: + $15,000 cash / + $15,000 notes payable.

3. Acme buys a $12,000 widget machine. Owes the machine supplier.
+ $12,000 fixed assets / + $12,000 accounts payable.

4. Acme buys $5,000 of raw materials. Owes the supplier.
+ $5,000 inventory—raw materials / + $5,000 accounts payable.

5. Acme rents space. Pays $250 for one month's rent in advance.
− $250 cash / + $250 prepaid expenses.

In this transaction the entries only affect the asset side of the balance sheet. Therefore, the worksheet must show a plus (+) and a minus (−) in order to maintain balance. (Transactions 3, 4, and 5 are shown in the balance sheet in Figure 3.)

6. The bank's note is repaid at the end of the six months. The worksheet might look like this:

6. Repay bank loan: − $15,000 cash / − $15,000 notes payable.

7. The machine is paid for: − $12,000 cash / − $12,000 accounts payable.
8. The raw materials are paid for: − $5,000 cash / − $5,000 accounts payable.
9. Raw materials for 40,000 more widgets are purchased. The raw materials cost $1.00 for each widget that can be made from them. When the year ends, we have not paid the supplier for the last order for raw materials for 10,000 widgets. The worksheet might look like this:

9. Purchase $40,000 raw materials, pay for $30,000:
      + $40,000 inventory—raw materials / − $30,000 cash /
      + $10,000 accounts payable.

This series of transactions requires more than one entry to arrive at a balance. This will often be true. Be sure that each part of a worksheet transaction balances by itself.

10. Enough raw materials for 41,000 widgets are manufactured into finished widgets ($41,000 worth).

. . . + $41,000 Inventory—finished goods /
            − $41,000 inventory—raw materials.

11. Acme sells 36,500 widgets at $2.00 each. During the year customers pay for 28,000 widgets. At year-end Acme is still owed for 8,500.

There are really several transactions here. Let's look at each one. First, there is a transaction affecting inventory.

36,500 widgets sold: − $36,500 inventory—finished goods / . . .

How do we balance this one? When we take the widgets out of inventory and ship them to customers, we have reduced the inventory asset by $36,500. Have we increased any other asset by a like amount? No, we have not. This transaction does not balance by increasing an asset.

Have we reduced any liability by $36,500 to balance the reduction in the asset? No, nothing like that has occurred.

Let's look at capital. Shipping off 36,500 widgets doesn't affect common stock. But the shipment does affect retained earnings. When we ship out 36,500 widgets, inventory is reduced by $36,500. Retained earnings are reduced by the same amount. The balance sheet continues to balance.

The shipment is a result of sales. The sales are for $73,000. The amount of $73,000 goes into accounts receivable since the customer owes us this amount for the shipment. We have increased the accounts receivable asset by $73,000. What balances this entry?

Did any other asset go down by this amount? No. Do we owe someone more money (did we add to our liabilities) as a result of this sale? No.

So once again we look to capital—specifically, to retained earnings.

Sales of $73,000: + $73,000 accounts receivable /
$\qquad$ + $73,000 retained earnings.

The next transaction occurs when customers pay for 28,000 of the 36,500 widgets. This results in $56,000 cash/ −$56,000 accounts receivable.

Note carefully. We ended up with a profit shown in retained earnings of $36,500—EVEN THOUGH we had collected no cash. When the cash was collected, it did not affect profits or retained earnings at all. Profits and retained earnings are not the same as cash.

12. We must depreciate the widget machine. We have determined that its useful life is ten years. At the end of ten years it will be worth nothing. It's original cost of $12,000 will be reduced to zero. We decide to depreciate the widget machine on a straight-line basis over ten years. This means that the depreciation will be the same for each month of the ten years. The monthly depreciation will be the original cost—$12,000—divided by the number of months of useful life, 120. So

the monthly depreciation is $100, and $1,200 for the year. This is entered into the worksheet as follows:

... — $12,000 depreciation of fixed assets /
                               — $1,200 retained earnings.

Again, we have an entry that is balanced by an effect upon profits and retained earnings. We have paid out the cash already. When the cash was paid to buy the machine it did not directly affect retained earnings. This was an expenditure, but it was not yet an expense. It is expenses that affect profits and retained earnings. Depreciation is an expense but the purchase of the fixed asset is not. It is an expenditure.

Depreciation is one of the more difficult accounting concepts. It is a means of charging the cost of a fixed asset such as a machine or a building to expense as the machine or building is being used. The expense is charged over the useful life of the asset. The IRS and experience set guidelines for what the useful life is. We know that a building usually lasts longer than a car. Buildings are usually depreciated over 20 to 40 years; cars over 3 or 4 years. (Of course, buildings can have useful lives of hundreds of years. Cars can last for ten or twenty years. But extreme cases are not the basis for depreciation.) Depreciation can be straight-line—the same amount of depreciation expense each period. Or depreciation can be accelerated with a greater depreciation expense in the early years of the asset's life, and less later on. In any case, depreciation cannot add up to more than the original cost. Some people view depreciation as a means of accumulating the money to buy a replacement for the machine, building, or whatever is being depreciated. This is not the purpose. Depreciation serves to change an expenditure, which does not affect profits and retained earnings, into an expense, which does. It is a means of getting the cost of a fixed asset off the balance sheet over a period of time as the asset is used.

Sales increase profits. Depreciation reduces profits and thereby reduces retained earnings on the balance sheet. Let's go on.

13. Acme rents space for $250 per month. Each month's rent is paid in advance. Transaction 5 recorded the payment of the first month's rent. This rent was rec-

orded as a prepaid expense. It was used up when Acme occupied the space for the month. Put this on your worksheet.

14. During the year, Acme pays rent each month. It makes twelve payments in addition to the one discussed above. Put these twelve rent payments on your worksheet. These payments affect three items on the balance sheet.

15. As owner-managers of Acme, you and I deserve a salary. Let's pay ourselves $1,000 a month each. We will get our salaries five days after the close of the month in which they are earned. Put this onto your worksheet. It affects three items.

16. Acme has postage, telephone, and other office expenses. They total $50 a month and are paid during the month. Put this on your worksheet.

17. Acme spends $2,000 to print an advertising circular promoting its widgets. An additional $500 is spent to mail the circular to prospective widget customers.

18. Acme owes $1,150 in income taxes on its profits from first-year operations. It won't have to pay these taxes until several months after year-end. When you put this on your worksheet, you have finished all of the transactions.

A "TRIAL BALANCE"

You should now have all of these 18 transactions recorded on your worksheet. Using these transactions, we are going to construct a balance sheet showing the financial position of Acme Widget Company at the end of its first year of operations.

It is difficult to go from the worksheet to the balance sheet. An intermediate step is a great help. Take another piece of paper. Also get a calculator or adding machine. It will speed your computations.

You can use any format that is convenient for you. I find the one shown in Figure 4 to be good for me. I go through the worksheet and enter onto my "trial balance" each entry. I put the entry under the appropriate heading with its plus or minus mark. For instance, the first transaction would be recorded as "+$20,000" under "Cash" and then "+$20,000" under "Common Stock."

Make your own trial balance worksheet. Fill it in.

Figure 4

Acme Widget Company—Trial Balance Worksheet

ASSETS

Cash	Accounts Receivable	Inventory Raw Materials	Inventory Finished Goods

Prepaid Expenses	Fixed Assets	Depreciation	
			TOTAL ASSETS

LIABILITIES

Accounts Payable	Notes Payable	Accruals	
			TOTAL LIABILITIES

CAPITAL

Common Stock	Retained Earnings	
		TOTAL CAPITAL

Mine shows total assets of $37,200. Total liabilities are $13,150. Total capital $24,050. What does yours show?

This is a trial balance, so go back and check it if it doesn't balance. (Don't forget: Assets = Liabilities + Capital.)

When you have things in balance—or when you are completely and hopelessly stumped—you can check out the worksheet I have prepared for myself. You can also see the "trial balance" worksheet I did. These are shown in the Appendix. If we don't agree, check carefully to see where you are making a mistake. Perhaps you didn't subtract depreciation from fixed assets. Or perhaps you need new batteries in your calculator.

CONSTRUCTING THE BALANCE SHEET

With the trial balance worksheet it is a simple matter to construct a balance sheet. Do one on a sheet of paper. Use this format:

ACME WIDGET COMPANY
Balance Sheet for the First Year of Operations

ASSETS	LIABILITIES
Cash	Accounts Payable
Accounts Receivable	Notes Payable
Inventory	Accruals
Raw Materials	Total Liabilities
Finished Goods	
Total	CAPITAL
Prepaid Expenses	Common Stock
Fixed Assets	Retained Earnings
Less Depreciation	Total Capital
Net Fixed Assets	
Total Assets	Total Liabilities and Capital

When you have finished constructing your balance sheet, you can compare it with one that I did. Mine is in the Appendix.

Acme Widget Company doesn't have much cash according to my figures. Is the company in big trouble? Or are they doing well for a new company? How much would you be willing to pay for Acme Widget Company at this point?

We will do some analysis of the balance sheet in the next chapter. Try to answer the questions asked above now. This will help you to see what kind of analysis might be needed.

SUMMARY

The balance sheet is a statement of a company's financial position at a moment in time. It shows the assets—all the things of value that a company owns—on the left-hand side. It shows the liabilities—what a company owes—on the right-hand side. Also on the right-hand side of the balance sheet is shown capital—the amounts invested and earned by the owners of the company. The total of the assets equals the total of the liabilities and capital. The formula is: Assets = Liabilities + Capital.

Principal assets we have covered are cash, accounts receivable, inventory, prepaid expenses, and fixed assets (less depreciation).

Principal liabilities we have covered are accounts payable, notes payable, and accruals. Principal capital items covered are common stock and retained earnings.

A balance sheet shows scores. The cash item is probably real. Normally it can be spent. Other items may or may not be what the numbers show. The accounts receivable may be owed by deadbeats who will never pay. The inventory may be out-of-date and unsalable. The machinery or other fixed assets may be obsolete or falling apart long before the so-called useful life is up.

On the other hand, assets purchased in prior years may be much more valuable today due to inflation. Any balance sheet is an estimate. The estimate can be more or less accurate, depending on many factors.

Whether the estimate is a good one or a bad one, the balance sheet must balance. Assets must equal liabilities plus capital. That's how the rules are set up for keeping this score.

4. More Balance Sheet

THIS CHAPTER continues the discussion of the balance sheet. We will introduce some new concepts and some new factors. But before we plunge back into the balance sheet itself, there are a few other items that need to be covered.

COST VS. VALUE

Items shown on the balance sheet are shown at original cost, unless they have been written down. This means that items go onto the balance sheet at their original cost. If something is purchased at an inflated cost, it goes on the balance sheet at that cost, even if it is actually worth much less.

If an asset is purchased at a great bargain and its value is really much greater than the cost, it will still go onto the balance sheet at its cost.

Assets may be reduced in value—written down—when the company wishes to recognize a loss in value. A loss in value may arise when a customer goes bankrupt and can't pay its bills. This customer's account receivable is not worth its original value.

Inventory may be reduced in value when it goes out of style or is replaced by a new model or can't be sold because of tough competition.

A fixed asset can be reduced in value, too. Perhaps it can no longer do the job. A buggy whip machine may operate perfectly to turn out buggy whips. But if there is no longer any demand for that product, then the value of a machine making that product may well be greatly reduced. It may be worth nothing but scrap value.

A complete loss of value results in a write-off. A reduction in value results in a write-down. Well-run and honest companies take their write-offs and write-downs as soon as the asset loses value. But some companies try to appear worth more than they really are. They do not take any write-downs or write-offs. Their assets may be shown at values far above their actual worth.

In analyzing any operation it is necessary to look at the asset side of the balance sheet. Consider whether or not the amounts shown are the true values. Perhaps they are overstated and write-downs or write-offs should be applied.

As a general rule of thumb, any company in serious financial difficulty is overstating the value of its assets. Accounts receivable may be worth 60 percent to 75 percent of what is shown. Inventory may only be worth ten cents for every dollar shown.

Of course, analysis can show hidden values. For example, a company balance sheet may show its factory and the adjacent land at the original cost of $150,000, less depreciation of the building. Meanwhile, the surrounding area has expanded rapidly. Raw land is selling for $2.00 per square foot. If the factory were torn down and the land sold, the company could get $1,650,000 for the property. Such a company's balance sheet would be greatly understating the true worth of its assets.

A balance sheet is not exact. It can reveal and it can hide. It is one of the primary means of keeping score in business, but the scores shown on the balance sheet must be analyzed.

INTANGIBLE ASSETS
Intangible assets are those assets that are not physical objects or tangible things like cash or accounts receivable. Patents and copyrights are good examples of intangible assets. Other examples are licenses, franchises, contracts, or other agreements which give a company valuable rights.

These kinds of assets lack the solid material substance of buildings or machines or goods in the warehouse. But they are certainly real. For many companies, intangible assets are the most valuable assets. The patent that gives a chemical company an exclusive monopoly on a valuable chemical may be that company's most valuable asset. Similarly, the copyrights that a publishing company controls give it the right to publish best-selling books, which can be the basis of the company's success.

A franchise for an exclusive territory, a license for a

process or a product, a marketing or distribution agreement, a long-term service contract—these are all valuable intangible assets.

BUT . . . many times these valuable assets do not appear on the balance sheet. There are sound tax reasons for not putting them on the balance sheet. Often there are other reasons as well. Almost every company has some important intangible assets that are not on the balance sheet.

The know-how and energy of the employees is an extremely important asset that is never shown on balance sheets. Of course, it is difficult to put a value on employee capability, but don't ignore it. Just because it is not listed on the balance sheet does not mean that it has no value.

The same is true of other intangible assets. One of my big mistakes was to value a potential acquisition in terms of assets shown on its balance sheet. The computer programs and data base of the company had cost hundreds of thousands of dollars to develop. They were a major asset of the company. But they were not shown on the balance sheet. My offer to purchase the company did not allow enough for this intangible but valuable asset that was not recorded. Another company made a better offer and made the acquisition.

When looking at the balance sheet of any company always ask: What assets vital to the success of the company are *not* shown on the balance sheet?

It is often wise to prepare a supplement to the balance sheet on which you list the important assets which the accountants have not shown on the balance sheet.

Sometimes, intangible assets are shown on the balance sheet. Then be cautious. Setting a value on intangible assets is often very difficult. Who really knows what a patent or a franchise is worth? This difficulty in valuation is one reason that accountants resist including intangible assets on balance sheets. A majority of companies prefer not to show most intangible assets. When a company does show significant intangible assets, my suspicious mind asks whether management is trying to pump up the value of the company with hot air.

There are two sides to the intangible asset coin. If a company lists them, they may be inflated. If they are not listed, then the company value may be understated.

GOODWILL

There is one special kind of intangible asset found on many balance sheets—goodwill. This is a special accounting term that does not mean the same thing it means to the layperson. This goodwill arises from acquisitions.

If Acme Widget were to acquire another company's assets, it would usually pay a price different from the value of those assets shown on the books of the selling company. Acme would pay more or less than the book value. You have seen that the values shown on the balance sheet are not necessarily the "true" values. They are unlikely to be the values on which a buyer and seller would agree.

If Acme paid more for the assets of another company than the book value of those assets, there is a problem. How does Acme account for the payment in excess of the book value? To keep the balance sheet in balance, the payment made must be balanced by the assets acquired. Since the payment is greater than the value of the assets, another kind of asset is invented to absorb the extra amount. This is goodwill.

Accountants invented goodwill to represent the excess of purchase price over book value. In some cases it really is goodwill—the reputation of a company and the goodwill of its customers. Such goodwill makes the other assets more valuable. This kind of goodwill is an intangible, but valuable asset.

In other cases, goodwill represents inflation which has not been recognized on the balance sheet. Or it may be the premium paid to buy out a competitor. Goodwill can arise from a number of circumstances. It represents an excess of cost paid over the book value of acquired assets.

Most executives do not like goodwill on their balance sheets. It just sits there. It cannot be used up like inventory. It cannot be depreciated like fixed assets. It does not represent anything concrete and it is an expenditure that cannot be recovered through use or depreciation. This means the IRS does not help to pay for goodwill. It cannot be written off against income to save taxes.

So in many acquisitions there is a great scrambling to find ways to reduce or eliminate goodwill. The IRS has plugged most palatable ways. So goodwill is often found on the balance sheets of companies.

When evaluating the worth of a company, it is usually safe to discount or even ignore the goodwill asset. However, the company may well have important hidden assets. The reputation and goodwill of its customers may be among these. But this is usually different from the goodwill shown on the balance sheet. Goodwill represents another reason to be cautious in interpreting and analyzing balance sheets.

RESERVES AND ALLOWANCES

Most balance sheets show reserves or allowances. These are reductions in the value of assets because of expected problems.

For example, most large companies find that a certain percent of their customers do not pay their bills. The company may not know how many dollars of uncollected accounts there will be in any given year. But an estimate can be made. From this estimate a reserve for doubtful accounts or an allowance for bad debts can be set up. This reserve or allowance is subtracted from the value of the accounts receivable.

Similarly, large inventories usually have some items that are not going to be able to be sold at full price. Perhaps they are out of style, obsolete, or have been damaged in the warehouse. The company may not know exactly how much the value of the total inventory should be reduced to allow for this. But an estimate can be made. A reserve or allowance for inventory obsolescence can be set up. This reserve or allowance will reduce the value of the inventory.

These are the two principal reserves or allowances. But any assets can have a reserve or allowance for possible loss in value. Even cash can lose value. Changes in foreign currency exchange rates can cause changes in the value of cash.

The setting up of a reserve or allowance reduces the value of an asset. The balance sheet must balance. So a corresponding entry must be made somewhere else. Where?

Setting up a reserve or allowance reduces an asset. It also reduces the owner's equity. Retained earnings are reduced to balance the reduction in the asset. Setting up a reserve or allowance creates no debt or obligation to pay someone. It doesn't increase the value of any other asset. So it must reduce retained earnings.

Any business of any size which shows no reserves or allowances may be overvaluing its assets. Watch for this.

The amount of reserves or allowances can be subject to bad estimates or just plain fudging. During recessions many companies find that they do not have enough reserves for bad debts. Rosy predictions of profits can be jolted when reserves have to be adjusted to reflect the actual situation.

THE GOING CONCERN ASSUMPTION

Almost every financial report you see is based on the assumption that the business will continue indefinitely. The going concern assumption is important. It may be false. If a business is about to go under, its assets will be worth a great deal less than if the business is to continue. A company going out of business finds it difficult to sell off its inventory. Sales efforts let down. Production quality controls slip. Certain items will be unavailable because depleted inventory won't be replenished. Customers often won't buy an incomplete line. Odd inventory items are only salable at deep discounts or on very liberal credit terms.

Shaky customers seldom bother to pay a company they won't be doing business with in the future. Bad debts shoot up.

For these and other reasons, the assets of a company going out of business are usually worth much less than if the company were to continue in business. Almost all financial reports assume that a company plans to stay in business—that it is a going concern.

ESTIMATES ARE EVERYWHERE

A great many numbers on financial reports are estimates. They are not exact amounts, even if the numbers show exact pennies. Reserves and allowances are estimates. Intangible assets shown on the balance sheet are surely estimated as to value.

Timing causes estimates to be made. Often the numbers for the last month are estimated since the management wants a twelve-month report before final results of the last month can be calculated. So estimates for the twelfth month are added to the actual figures for the preceding eleven months.

Many numbers on financial reports are estimates. Some are very close to actual. Some are not so close. Some estimates are made to be as close to the actual as possible. Some estimates are made to conceal the likely truth. There are rosy estimates and gloomy estimates. Each has its purposes.

Always be aware that at least part of any financial report is made up of estimates, not real, actual, "true" figures. Where estimates speed up useful management reports, they can be good. Where they are used to obscure the true situation, they can be bad.

PURPOSE AND PERSPECTIVE

Accounting serves different purposes. Financial reports are viewed from different perspectives. The balance sheet for the same time for the same company may have different versions.

The reports prepared for the tax authorities may be different from the reports prepared for the shareholders. The reports for tax purposes may minimize profits so as to minimize taxes. The reports for shareholders may maximize profits to make the company's stock appear more valuable.

Accountants can treat the same transaction in different ways to arrive at different results. For example, depreciation might be straight-line or it might be accelerated. Footnotes will usually tell of the existence of different financial reports or different methods of computing profits and asset values. Whenever thy appear, ALWAYS read the footnotes to financial reports.

This is important enough to repeat. *Always read the footnotes to financial reports.*

If there are two different financial reports for the same company for the same period, which one is the true report?

By now your answer should be, "neither one; it depends."

There is no such thing as the "true" financial report. Each report is true—insofar as the estimates and assumptions are true, and insofar as it is true to the purpose for which it is intended.

Whether or not a financial report is true for you depends upon your perspective. Are you looking at the report as one of the company's managers? As a tax agent? As a potential acquirer? As an investor in the company's stock? As a person considering employment with the company? Each perspective calls for a financial report that may differ from others if a picture most useful to that perspective is to be shown.

If I were to choose one financial report as "true," it is the one that is most conservative and cautious in valuing assets. This is often the report prepared for tax purposes. When looking at a potential acquisition, I always try to examine the tax returns. These numbers can be weighed against numbers shown in other reports.

Purpose and perspective affect the numbers shown on financial reports.

We began this chapter discussing original cost vs. value. We went from there to intangible assets with a special look at goodwill. Then reserves and allowances were discussed. The going business assumption was presented. Then we saw that balance sheets and other financial reports contain many estimates and can vary depending upon purpose and perspective. The thrust of all of these points has been to undermine the idea that there is such a thing as a "true" financial report that completely and accurately reflects the status of a company.

Before we get back to the actual balance sheet itself, we need to present some other concepts.

CURRENT VS. NON-CURRENT BALANCE SHEET ITEMS

Most balance sheets are divided into current and non-current sections. Current assets include all assets that can be expected to turn into cash within a short period of time—usually a year. Included in current assets are cash, marketable securities, accounts receivable, inventories, and prepaid expenses or deferred charges likely to be used up in a year or less.

Current liabilities are normally those that will be paid off in a short time—a year or less. Included in current liabilities are accounts payable, notes payable within a year, accrued expenses and taxes, and that portion of long-term debt due within the next twelve months—the current installments due.

Non-current assets are those not likely to be converted to cash quickly. Fixed assets are the major non-current assets. Goodwill and other intangible assets are also non-current.

Non-current or long-term liabilities include all long-term debt such as bonds, term loans, and mortgages. However, the installments due on this debt within the next twelve months are considered a current liability.

Capital is non-current.

WORKING CAPITAL

Working capital is one of the most commonly used scores. Working capital equals current assets minus current liabilities. Theoretically, working capital is the capital in the business that is working on a day-by-day basis to produce the profits.

Look at the first-year balance sheet for Acme Widget. Use your own or the one in the Appendix. Identify and total up the current assets. Then identify and total up the current liabilities. Calculate Acme's working capital by subtracting the current liabilities from the current assets.

As a business grows it needs more working capital. As sales expand, customers owe the business more money. Accounts receivable grow. Inventory usually must grow, too, to accommodate a growth in sales. The growth of accounts receivable and inventory expands current assets. Where does the money come from for this?

The company is likely to owe its suppliers more as it buys more inventory. So the suppliers help to finance some of the growth of assets. The company may accrue larger payrolls and other expenses. Current liabilities grow. Often short-term loans are borrowed from the bank to help meet the need for expanded working capital.

Current liabilities can almost never grow as fast as current assets grow when a company is expanding sales. So the growth in working capital needed to support sales growth must be financed from some other source. Remember that the balance sheet must balance. If current assets go up faster than current liabilities, then long-term liabilities or capital must increase.

Profits are the major source for financing increases in current assets. The company takes its after-tax profits and plows them back into the business rather than paying out the profits as dividends.

Other sources of financing for working capital increases are long-term loans or the sale of additional stock.

Sometimes none of these sources are available. Money may be tight and banks or other lenders reluctant to lend. The stock market may be depressed and no stock can be sold. Profits may be inadequate to finance working capital needs. When these situations occur a company can literally expand into bankruptcy.

This is an important concept. Learn it well. You can go broke when your sales are growing by leaps and bounds. I have acquired several companies that suffered this fate. I have seen many others liquidated or swallowed up.

How can a growing company go broke? Easy.

As sales grow and grow, more and more of the company's funds are tied up in accounts receivable and inventory. Cash to buy new inventory begins to run dry. Suppliers refuse to ship until accounts payable are paid. They refuse to extend further credit. Banks, insurance companies, and other lenders refuse to give the company any more loans. No new money can be raised from stockholders. Profits are insufficient to handle the growth of working capital needs.

The more sales the company makes, the more trouble it gets into. It must buy inventory to fill the new orders and then wait until customers get around to paying. If money is tight all over, customers start slowing down their payments. Eventually, the company actually runs out of cash. It cannot come up with the money to pay suppliers, employees, tax collectors, and so forth.

Sometimes the outcome is delayed by the company borrowing money at very high interest rates. But the high interest usually eats up the profits that might be used to expand working capital.

A famous promoter once said he would rather be alive at high interest rates. He went bankrupt anyway.

What can a company do when it is successful in sales and going broke at the same time? Simple. Stop expanding working capital faster than it can be financed.

Collect accounts receivable faster with a tougher collection effort. Cut off credit to slow-paying customers. Demand cash with orders. Shift the sales and advertising efforts to customers who will pay quickly.

Look for ways to move inventory in and out more quickly. Companies are often organized so that there is a long lag from the time they buy inventory until they sell finished goods. Inventory is money. The longer it takes inventory to flow through the business, the longer money is tied up and unavailable. The ideal goal is to sell inventory so fast that you collect from your customers before you have to pay your suppliers. Most companies can't do things this fast. But every company can find ways to speed inventory turnover.

The first way to control working capital is to get hold of the key assets. Accounts receivable must be held in check. Inventory must move rapidly. It often happens that controlling assets slows down sales growth. So be it. Selling more and more to get deeper and deeper into the hole is dumb.

After assets are controlled, you can look to liabilities. If the problem is temporary, perhaps a short-term loan can help. But don't kid yourself. Usually working capital problems are long-term.

Talk to your suppliers. Can you temporarily slow down payments to get a breather? Perhaps a different supplier will give you easier credit terms.

Don't fool with accruals. Delaying payments due to employees or governments is sure trouble. Desperate managers are tempted to use the dollars that are supposed to be withheld for social security or income taxes. Desperate managers like this often go to jail.

Working capital problems are rarely, if ever, solved by fiddling with liabilities. Holding down on current assets is the primary solution.

Many smaller companies are headed by sales wizards. They really know how to generate sales. But they often get into trouble. Sales wizards usually think that more sales will cure any problem. But working capital problems seldom succumb to more sales. More sales can make the problem worse. And the sales wizard ends up having to sell his company to a larger, richer company that can balance sales with profits and working capital requirements. The sales wizard can't understand what happened to his company. It was going so great.

I hope this is clear. A company that is successful in sales can go broke. Sales must be turned into profits. Sales must be supported by adequate working capital, which is normally built up by profits. If sales grow faster than profits or working capital, a seemingly successful company can go sour.

AVERAGE COLLECTION PERIOD

In discussing working capital problems we touched upon the problems of collecting accounts receivable. Now let's look at a useful way to measure trends in collections.

The average collection period is the number of days required, on average, to collect amounts owed to the company by its customers. A company that collects cash when it makes a sale has an advantage over a company that has to wait six months to get paid. A company that took twenty days, on the average, to collect its accounts last year and which takes thirty days this year, has a problem. If its customers normally owe it $1 million, the extra ten days for collection mean that the company is denied the use of $1 million in cash for ten days.

The average collection period is expressed in days. It is computed as follows:

$$\text{Average Collection Period} = \frac{\text{Average Accounts Receivable}}{\text{Annual Sales}} \times 365$$

If Acme Widget had average accounts receivable of $20,000 and annual sales of $100,000, the equation would look like this.

$$\text{Average Collection Period} = \frac{20,000}{100,000} \times 365 =$$

73 days Average Collection Period

What if the next year, Acme Widget had sales of $120,-000 and average accounts receivable of $25,000. What would the average collection period be? Is this better or worse than the previous year?

A lengthening of the average collection period can indicate that a company is getting into working capital troubles.

Each industry and each company has its own typical average collection period—normally a range within which the average days fall. A grocery store that sells only for cash has zero days average collection period. Businesses that sell large items to governments face much red tape in getting paid. The average collection period for such businesses may extend into many months.

The trend is what is important to a company. An average collection period that is getting longer must be watched. The average collection period can be shortened by collecting accounts more aggressively, by tightening up on credit terms, or by shifting sales efforts away from slower-paying customers.

A trend toward a longer average collection period may indicate a slackening collection effort. Goods may be sold to less credit-worthy customers. The trend may also indicate that a fading product line, or a weak sales effort, or tough new competition make it much more difficult to get sales without giving extended credit as an inducement.

The average collection period is a valuable signal. It is well worth watching in your own business or in one you are considering.

INVENTORY TURNOVER

Inventory turnover is another signal that may warn of trouble ahead. We have said that inventory is money sitting in the factory or warehouse. Inventory sitting idle costs money. It costs the interest on the money used to purchase it. It costs the profits that might be made if the money could be used elsewhere.

Idle inventory costs money for storage, for rent, heat, power, security, and so forth. Various management consulting groups have determined that inventory sitting around idle costs from 20 to 25 percent of its original value each year. This is the combined cost of interest on money, space and other storage charges, and the inevitable deterioration or obsolescence of the inventory.

Inventory should move in and out quickly. How quickly depends on the industry and the company. A store specializing in crispy fresh produce or baked goods needs to move its inventory in and out in a day.

A company making complex heavy machinery may get raw materials or parts many, many months before the completed machinery is finally shipped to the customer.

Inventory turnover is a measure of how many times (theoretically) the inventory of a company is replenished during a year. The formula for calculating inventory turnover is this:

$$\text{Inventory Turnover} = \frac{\text{Cost of Sales}}{\text{Average Inventory}}$$

(See the Glossary for a definition of Cost of Sales. This will also be discussed in greater detail in later chapters.)

One of the problems in calculating inventory turnover (or average collection period) is getting the average. If you have monthly reports for a year, then add the numbers for each month and divide by 12. If you have quarterly reports, total the numbers and divide by four. Often the only thing available is an annual report. Take the number at the beginning of the year (or at the end of the previous year—same thing) and add it to the number at the end of the year. Then divide this sum by two.

What if only the one year-end number is available? Then use that. But be cautious. An average compiled from twelve monthly numbers is more useful than an average compiled from beginning and ending. The latter average cannot take into account possible huge variations during the year.

Still, the important thing about inventory turnover, as with average collection period, is the trend. Trends can often be spotted from very sparse data. Then further investigation can dig into the meaning of the trend.

If Acme Widget had a cost of sales during the year of $36,500, and an average inventory of $7,300 what would its inventory turnover be?

Suppose that during the next year, cost of sales went up to $75,000 and average inventory was $12,500. Would the second year inventory turnover indicate a better or poorer use of the money invested in inventory?

One more thing needs to be said about inventory turnover. For most companies, a few items produce the majority of sales. (See 80—20 rule in the Glossary.) This means that the inventory of a few items is probably turning over very rapidly. The inventory of a large number of items may be moving very slowly. Often the slow-moving inventory sits so long it becomes obsolete. If there are enough sales and a fast enough turnover from the hot items, the overall inventory turnover figure may look reasonable. Serious problems of slow-moving or even dead inventory can be obscured.

Inventory turnover is a useful trend indicator. But it cannot tell the whole story. To really analyze a business you need to get behind inventory turnover to see what is happening to individual items. Nevertheless, the inventory turnover figure can be a help in signaling possible trouble ahead.

In this section of this chapter we have introduced current and non-current balance sheet items. The concept of working capital was presented with the warning that working capital problems can sink companies with rapid sales growth.

We have just finished introducing two signals or trend indicators—average collection period and inventory turnover.

While we have been exploring these side paths, Acme Widget Company has been going forward. The company has now completed its second year of operations. It is time to prepare another balance sheet and then to apply some analysis.

5. Still More Balance Sheet

YOU ARE going to be the Acme Widget amateur accountant. You will prepare the balance sheet for the second year. You will follow the same procedures followed for the first year balance sheet.

I will give you the pertinent transactions that occurred during Acme operations in the second year. You will prepare a worksheet that records these transactions, showing each one's affect on the balance sheet—and by all means, keeping each transaction in balance.

From your worksheet you will prepare a trial balance worksheet. This will put each of the numbers under the appropriate balance sheet heading. Then you can add and subtract to see if the assets balance the liabilities and capital. When you have things in balance, then you can prepare a balance sheet.

So get out enough paper for your worksheets and balance sheet. Get out your calculator to do the arithmetic.

Figure 5 shows you the format for the Acme Widget balance sheet you are going to prepare. This format lists all of the items or entries you will be concerned with. You will also notice that this is a comparative balance sheet. The numbers at the end of the year are shown alongside the numbers for the end of year two. This allows a comparison of the financial position at these two times.

THE WORKSHEET FOR TRANSACTIONS

Look at the worksheet prepared at the end of year one. This will refresh your memory on how a worksheet is put together. The transactions at the end of year two will often be more complicated. Some of the transactions should be broken down into separate parts in order to keep them straight. Remember that each entry into the worksheet

62

Figure 5

ACME WIDGET COMPANY
BALANCE SHEET
Second Year of Operations

ASSETS	Year Two	Year One	LIABILITIES AND CAPITAL	Year Two	Year One
CURRENT ASSETS			**CURRENT LIABILITIES**		
Cash			Accounts Payable		
Marketable Securities			Accruals		
Accounts Receivable			Total Current Liabilities		
Less Reserve for					
Doubtful Accounts			**LONG-TERM LIABILITIES**		
Net Accounts Receivable			Long-Term Debt		
Inventory			Total Long-Term Liabilities		
Raw Materials					
Finished Goods			TOTAL LIABILITIES		
Total Inventory					
Prepaid Expenses					
Total Current Assets			CAPITAL		
			Common Stock		
NON-CURRENT ASSETS			Retained Earnings		
Fixed Assets					
Less Depreciation			TOTAL CAPITAL		
Net Fixed Assets					
Intangible Assets					
Total Non-Current Assets			TOTAL LIABILITIES		
TOTAL ASSETS			AND CAPITAL		

must balance. A change on one side of the balance sheet must be balanced by a corresponding change on the opposite side or by an offsetting change on the same side.

Sometimes, two or more changes will be needed to balance one change. You will get the hang of it as we go along.

1. In the second year Acme Widget sells 75,000 widgets at $2.00 each for total sales of $150,000. (On the worksheet I enter this information as two entries. First, I show the sales dollars added to accounts receivable, balanced by an equivalent amount entered as an addition to retained earnings. Then I deal with the withdrawal of the 75,000 units from inventory, reducing inventory—finished goods and correspondingly reducing retained earnings.)

2. Acme collects the accounts receivable owed to it at

the end of year one. It also collects 80 percent of the accounts receivable from sales during the second year. At year-end, the company is still owed $30,000. In examining the accounts, Acme management sees that certain customers have not paid for many months. It is decided to set up a reserve for doubtful accounts. The amount of the reserve is set up at 5 percent of the outstanding accounts receivable at year-end. (A reserve is a reduction.)

3. Acme purchases enough raw materials to make 87,500 widgets. Raw materials cost $1.00 per widget. The amount owed the supplier at the end of year one is paid. However, the last order for raw materials placed in year two—worth $12,500—has not been paid for when the year ends.

4. A widget machine operator is hired at the beginning of the second year. He is paid $700 a month. The Acme Widget owner-managers continue to pay themselves salaries of $1,000 a month each during year two. When the year ends, the last month's payroll has not been paid. (But remember that the payroll that was unpaid at the end of year one was paid early in year two.)

5. The widget machine operator makes 76,500 widgets during year two.

6. At the end of the second month of year two Acme Widget purchases used office furniture for $840. This will be depreciated over a seven-year period, straight-line depreciation (same amount each month).

7. In looking over the inventory at the end of the year it is found that mice have been chewing at the raw materials. Estimated loss is $200. It is also found that one style of widgets is no longer in demand. The inventory on hand can only be sold at greatly reduced prices, if at all. Acme Widget management decides to write off 1,000 widgets to no value. The cost of the raw materials in the 1,000 widgets is reduced to zero value in the inventory.

8. Acme Widget has an opportunity to buy the building it is occupying. The owner is willing to sell for $30,-000. She wants a down payment of $10,000. Then she will take back a mortgage for the remaining $20,000 to be paid over ten years at 9 percent interest. The deal is consummated at the end of the sixth month of

year two. Up until then Acme has been paying rent.
The deal provides that for the first year after the purchase Acme will pay interest only. Then principal payments will begin with interest paid on the outstanding
balance. The Acme owners each put $5,000 additional
into the company to provide cash for the down payment. For their additional investment they receive
more common stock. The Acme owners are delighted
with this deal. The building has some problems, but
they can live with it. They determine that the building
can be depreciated over a period of 25 years, straight
line. Depreciation begins when the deal is made. The
entire purchase price is depreciated, including the
mortgage. (This transaction is a bit complicated. You
may have to go over it a couple of times to figure out
the various worksheet entries involved. I make no
apology for this complexity. Most real-life business
transactions are more complicated.)

9. Acme Widget incurs a number of expenses during the
   year:
   a. Office expenses of $50 per month.
   b. Advertising during the year—$3,000. Paid for dur-
      ing the year. (You will recognize that Acme would
      have many more expenses. But we need not in-
      clude everything to make this learning exercise use-
      ful.)

10. During the year, Acme Widget purchases a license to
    a widget-making patent. The process it acquires
    through the license will improve product quality. A
    one-time payment of $1,500 is made for the license.

11. Seeing that the year is going to be profitable, the
    owners of Acme decide to pay a dividend. The Direc-
    tors declare a dividend of ten cents per share to be
    paid before the year ends. With the new stock issued,
    there are 30,000 shares outstanding. (Dividend pay-
    ments affect retained earnings.)

12. Acme feels that it has some excess cash as the year
    draws to a close. The company buys a certificate of
    deposit (CD) from the bank. This $1,000 CD will
    pay Acme interest and Acme can cash in the CD
    anytime after sixty days.

13. Don't forget that the depreciation continues on the
    widget machine purchased in year one. Depreciation is
    straight line.

14. Income taxes are due. The taxes due on the year one profits must be paid during year two.
15. Acme makes a profit from its operations in year two. (You can figure out that profit by looking at the retained earnings account.) Taxes of $9,150 will be due in year three.

This completes the transactions that need to be entered into your worksheet for Acme Widget's second year. Go over your entries again. Does each one balance?

When you are satisfied, you can check your worksheet against mine. But I recommend that you wait until you prepare your trial balance worksheet. Find out if you can make it balance. Then check. My worksheets can be found in the Appendix.

TRIAL BALANCE WORKSHEET

Look at the trial balance worksheet prepared at the end of Acme's first year. This will provide the format. Of course, you should have some additional headings. Look at Figure 5 to see what headings will be needed for your trial balance worksheet.

When you have the trial balance worksheet laid out, put in the numbers shown at the end of year one. For example, you don't start your Cash with nothing. There was $650 in the bank account at the end of the year one. Any additions and subtractions to cash in year two will be added to or subtracted from the $650 you begin with.

The same is true of other items. Begin with the amount in that item at the end of year one. Then enter the amounts from year two, showing them as plus or minus. Then add and subtract to get a total for each item. Then add up to see if they balance. If they do, you are ready to prepare the comparative balance sheet.

When you have finished your trial balance worksheet, it will balance or it won't. If assets equal liabilities plus capital on the first try, you are doing excellent work. Perhaps you should be an accountant.

If you are like most people, it won't balance. Then you should go back over the transaction worksheet and the trial balance worksheet to see what you may have missed. It may be helpful to compute the difference between assets and liabilities plus capital. That difference may be a number that indicates exactly what you left out.

Keep at it until you have the trial balance in balance— or until you are completely stumped. Then check your work against mine in the Appendix.

THE BALANCE SHEET

Now let's finish the job by preparing the comparative balance sheet or statement of Acme's financial position. If you own this book you might want to go back to Figure 5. Write in the numbers in the appropriate spaces. If this isn't your book, please don't spoil it for the next reader. Prepare a balance sheet on a separate piece of paper.

When you have finished you can check your balance sheet against mine. Mine is in the Appendix. When you are satisfied that you have a complete and accurate balance sheet we will do some analysis. After all, that's what all these numbers are really for—to help us make better judgments. Analysis of the financial reports is the basis for judgments.

We will use the Acme Widget balance sheet for year two to do several kinds of analysis and to make some judgments about the company. So go to it and finish up the balance sheet work.

ANALYZING THE BALANCE SHEET

You are an owner of Acme Widget. Let us suppose that a large conglomerate has offered to buy Acme for cash. How much cash would you want to get to sell Acme?

Your total capital (common stock plus retained earnings) is $53,900. This is the net worth of the company, according to the balance sheet. Would you sell the company for this amount? If not, how much would you be willing to sell it for?

In considering this question, you will want to think about what hidden assets, if any, Acme has that make it more valuable than the books show. What other factors might influence your decision on the value of Acme? For one thing, there is your own personal involvement in the company. That would certainly be changed if you sold out.

You can think of other considerations that would affect your analysis of the worth of Acme. The balance sheet does not tell the whole story.

Let's put the shoe on the other foot. You represent the large conglomerate. Your board of directors has instructed you to make a cash offer to acquire Acme Widget. You have the balance sheet in front of you. Now you must determine what would be a fair offer for the company.

You will not only want to identify hidden assets, but you will also want to consider possible hidden liabilities. Perhaps some of the assets are overvalued. It is clear that you will probably end up with a different value when you are a buyer than when you are a seller. Remember that perspective influences valuation. The scores that show on the financial reports do not represent an exact and "true" value.

Let's make some calculations. First, working capital (current assets minus current liabilities). What was the working capital of Acme at the end of year one? What is it at the end of year two?

The working capital has increased substantially. This is a natural enough result of the large increase in sales—from $73,000 in year one to $150,000 in year two. Has the increase in working capital been proportional to the increase in sales? Calculate the percentage growth in sales and then the percentage growth in working capital. This will show the answer.

Another approach is to calculate what percentage of sales the first year-end working capital was. Then calculate what percentage of second year sales the second year-end working capital was. You will find that the working capital at the end of the second year was a high percentage of sales. Is this important? It might be. If working capital as a percentage of sales continues to increase, the company could get into serious working capital problems if sales keep leaping upward.

Now let's compute the average collection period for Acme Widget. Use the beginning and ending accounts receivable for each year to calculate the average accounts receivable.

Which direction is the average collection period going? Is it getting shorter or longer? The company set up a reserve for doubtful accounts. What concerns would you want to express to the mangement from these signals?

There are additional aspects of the balance sheet that can be analyzed. Is the inventory worth what is shown? What possible problems might make the inventory less valuable?

The fixed assets have been depreciated. Is the depreciation shown a true indicator of the loss of value of these assets? How might the value of these fixed assets be different than what the balance sheet shows?

The owners of Acme put $30,000 in cash into the business. They have retained earnings of $23,900 after the end of two years of operation. How much cash do they have? Is there any relationship between retained earnings and cash?

We will come back to the balance sheet later on as we tie it into the analysis arising out of other kinds of financial reports.

BALANCE SHEET SUMMARY

It is time to wind up this discussion of the balance sheet with a summary of all that we have learned.

A balance sheet is a statement of the financial position of a company at a specific point in time.

The balance sheet is divided into three sections—assets, liabilities, and capital. Normally, assets are shown on the left-hand side or at the top. Liabilities and capital are shown on the right-hand side or on the lower part of the balance sheet.

The total of the assets must equal or balance the total of the liabilities and capital. If assets increase, then either liabilities or capital must correspondingly increase. The balance sheet formula is Assets = Liabilities + Capital.

Current assets are those that are likely to be converted into cash within one year. The assets are listed in the order that reflects their likelihood of conversion to cash.

Principal current assets are:

Cash—money on hand or in the bank checking account.

Marketable securities—short-term investments, easily converted to cash, usually used to earn interest on cash not immediately needed.

Accounts receivable—amounts owed to the company by its customers.

Reserve or allowance for doubtful accounts or bad debts —an amount set aside from accounts receivable to prepare or allow for estimated non-payment by customers.

Inventory—the store of raw materials, goods being manufactured, and finished goods ready for sale that a company has.

*Reserve for inventory loss, write-downs, write-offs—*amounts set aside from the inventory that represent estimated losses in inventory value due to deterioration, damage, obsolescence, or other causes.

*Prepaid expenses or deferred charges—*amounts paid in advance for goods or services that will come to the company in the future.

Non-current assets include:

*Fixed assets—*buildings, land, improvements to property, machinery, furniture, fixtures, vehicles, and equipment used in the business which have a useful life of more than a year—usually several years.

*Depreciation—*a reduction in the value of fixed assets to account for wear and tear and use. The actual amount of depreciation is controlled by IRS guidelines and is not necessarily related to the actual loss in value of the asset. Depreciation converts an expenditure to an expense.

Intangible assets—(these may appear under various names.) Included are items such as research and development expenditures, patents, copyrights, franchises, and licenses. Intangible assets are often not shown on the balance sheet, even though they may be important items of value.

*Goodwill—*the excess of the cost of assets acquired over their book value.

Assets are put on a company's books and entered onto the balance sheet at their original cost. This may or may not reflect the true value of the assets.

Liabilities are amounts owed by the company to other companies or individuals.

Liabilities are listed on the balance sheet in the approximate order in which they are likely to come due. Current liabilities come due within one year or less.

Principal current liabilities:

*Notes payable—*amounts owed to banks or other lenders due in a year or less. Short-term borrowings.

Current portion of long-term debt—the portion of the long-term debt which is due to be paid within a year or less—usually included in current liabilities.

Accounts payable—amounts owed to outside suppliers of goods or services.

Accruals—payroll, taxes, and other amounts that have been accrued or built up but that are not due to be paid until after the end of the accounting period.

Non-current liabilities include long-term debt, bonds, mortgages, and other debts owed to outside lenders and due over a period of several years.

Capital represents the owner's interest in a company. Capital is usually divided into two main categories:

Stock—common stock or preferred stock, shares of which have been issued in exchange for an investment.

Retained earnings—The owner's share of the success or failure of the company. Retained earnings are what is left over to balance the balance sheet when all other items are set down. Retained earnings represent all of the net profits made by the company after taxes, less any dividends paid.

The owner's interest in a company is also called the equity or the net worth. Net worth is total assets minus total liabilities—the capital. Net worth divided by the number of shares of common stock outstanding gives book value per share.

Working capital is current assets minus current liabilities. It represents the amount of day-to-day investment a company needs to finance its ongoing operations.

When the need for working capital expands faster than funds can be obtained from profits, loans, or selling stock, a company can go broke—even though its sales are growing. Companies with rapidly expanding sales can go into bankruptcy. Control of the growth of current assets, especially accounts receivable and inventory, is necessary to avoid this.

Average Collection Period =
$$\frac{\text{Average Accounts Receivable}}{\text{Sales}} \times 365$$

This is a trend indicator. It reflects the number of days needed to collect accounts receivable. If the number of days is increasing a company can get into serious cash trouble.

$$\text{Inventory Turnover} = \frac{\text{Cost of Sales}}{\text{Average Inventory}}$$

This is also a trend indicator. It reflects the velocity with which the inventory investment is being recycled. A slow turnover requires a larger investment than a fast turnover.

Now let's look at some of the other important ideas introduced.

Going concern—financial reports are based on the assumption that the company will keep on operating in the future with no dramatic shifts or changes. If this assumption is incorrect, the numbers on financial reports are likely to be much less meaningful or relevant.

Estimates—financial reports are based on many estimates. Some numbers are exact, but a significant portion are estimates. If the estimates are shaky, the financial reports are shaky.

No "true" financial reports—there is no one single "true" and accurate financial report for all purposes and perspectives. The same company for the same period can show different profits, different asset values, and different net worth, depending on the way the financial reports are prepared. Estimates affect this. Equally important, the purpose for which the financial report is prepared affects the numbers.

Hidden assets and liabilities—some important things are not shown. Financial reports can never show all of the important facts about a company. There are always hidden assets. There are hidden liabilities. Factors such as the quality of the staff, market share, potential new technology, competition, impending government regulations, and so forth are not shown on balance sheets but can have a profound impact upon a company's status.

We are now finished with the balance sheet—and much else. You have completed the most difficult part of this book. Congratulations!

What follows will build upon the foundation of the balance sheet. With what you now know, other financial reports will be much easier to understand. You have learned the first and most important lessons on how to keep score in business.

And by now you well understand that financial reports are better at reflecting scores than they are at showing real dollar values.

6. The Income Statement

THE INCOME STATEMENT summarizes the results of a company's operations over a period of time. It is also called the profit and loss statement, the operating statement, statement of earnings, and other names. It is the financial report that shows the bottom line—net profit after taxes.

The balance sheet shows the company's financial position at one point in time—say at the close of business on 31 December. The income statement summarizes the financial results of operations over a period of time—say from 1 January through 31 December. The income statement can show the result of operations for a day, a week, a month, a quarter, a year, or any period of time.

The income statement is the financial report most often used by managers in business. When financial plans and budgets are prepared, the income statement format is usually the principal one used. In many management positions the balance sheet is almost never referred to. All of the financial information is centered around the income statement.

If this is so, you may wonder why we spent so much time introducing the balance sheet. Why did we start with it rather than with the income statement?

As we discuss the income statement you will see that it flows from the balance sheet. The understandings you developed in your study of the balance sheet will make it far easier to understand what is shown—and what is not shown—on the income statement. Like the balance sheet, the income statement is a score-keeping device. The numbers shown are not necessarily true, nor do they necessarily represent real dollars. Your work with the balance sheet will make it easier for you to understand this.

In this chapter we will dissect the income statement into its component parts. We will start simply and progress toward the more complex. Several Acme Widget income statements will be constructed. Then we will do some analysis.

First, let's look at some typical corporate income statements. Get a general impression of them. After you have finished this chapter, you will want to come back to these real-life income statements and study and analyze them more carefully.

As you look at these income statements you will notice that they begin with sales. They all end with net profit after taxes, or income. In between the sales and the net profit are all the expenses incurred by the company during the period covered by the income statement.

THE BASIC INCOME STATEMENT

Basically, an income statement has four main sections—sales, expenses, taxes, and profits. Sales minus expenses minus taxes equals profits.

Let's illustrate this (and some other important ideas) by preparing an income statement for Acme Widget's first month of operation. The following transactions occurred:

1. Cash was put into the business in exchange for stock. This has no effect upon the income statement.
2. $15,000 was borrowed from the bank. This has no effect upon the income statement.
3. A widget machine was purchased for $12,000. This has no effect upon the income statement.
4. An initial order of raw material was purchased. The supplier was not paid. These transactions have no effect upon the income statement.

We had better stop here for a moment. All of these activities went on, involving large sums of money. Yet none of them show up on the income statement. They all affect the balance sheet. This is because expenses are different from expenditures. (See Glossary.)

An expenditure usually occurs when money changes hands. But an expense occurs when an expenditure is recorded so as to affect a company's profits. This often happens at a different time than the expenditure.

The expenditure was made by Acme for the widget machine and for the raw materials when these things were

The Coca-Cola Company and Subsidiaries
Consolidated Statements of Profit and Loss

	YEAR ENDED DECEMBER 31,	
	1977	1976
Net sales....................................	$3,559,878,282	$3,094,523,628
Cost of goods sold.........................	2,009,700,447	1,728,960,485
GROSS PROFIT...........................	1,550,177,835	1,365,563,143
Selling, administrative and general expenses....	957,072,552	837,857,757
OPERATING PROFIT......................	593,105,283	527,705,386
Other income..............................	42,871,486	47,052,697
	635,976,769	574,758,083
Less other deductions......................	30,634,018	29,232,022
PROFIT BEFORE TAXES ON INCOME......	605,342,751	545,526,061
Provision for taxes on income...............	279,123,000	254,809,937
NET PROFIT.............................	$ 326,219,751	$ 290,716,124
Net profit per share of common stock.........................	$2.67	$2.38

Consolidated Statements of Earned Surplus

	YEAR ENDED DECEMBER 31,	
	1977	1976
Balance at January 1:		
The Coca-Cola Company and Subsidiaries	$1,266,268,875	$1,096,716,913
The Taylor Wine Company, Inc...............		40,365,750
Adjusted balance at January 1.................		1,137,082,663
Net profit for the year.......................	326,219,751	290,716,124
Dividends paid in cash:		
The Coca-Cola Company (per share— 1977, $1.54; 1976, $1.325)...............	188,170,329	158,787,031
The Taylor Wine Company, Inc., prior to combination...........................		2,742,881
BALANCE AT DECEMBER 31	$1,404,318,297	$1,266,268,875

See Notes to Consolidated Financial Statements

Consolidated Statements of Operations and Retained Earnings

	1977	1976
Net sales	$31,131,978	$29,501,606
Cost of sales	24,765,462	21,862,324
Gross profit on sales	6,366,516	7,639,282
Selling, shipping, general and administrative expenses	6,060,445	5,674,445
	306,071	1,964,837
Other expenses (income):		
Loss (gain) on disposal of property, plant and equipment	4,917	(164,866)
Interest expense	551,665	580,727
Other, principally interest income in 1976	(21,941)	(80,854)
	534,641	335,007
(Loss) income before income taxes and extraordinary credit	(226,570)	1,629,830
(Credit) provision for Federal and state income taxes:		
Current	(141,000)	633,000
Deferred	21,000	32,000
	(120,000)	665,000
(Loss) income before extraordinary credit	(106,570)	964,830
Extraordinary credit—Federal income tax benefit of loss carryforward	—	72,000
Net (loss) income	(106,570)	1,036,830
Retained Earnings at beginning of year	4,657,545	3,620,715
Retained Earnings at end of year—Note E	$ 4,548,975	$ 4,657,545
(Loss) income per common and common equivalent share—Note I:		
Income (loss) before extraordinary credit	$(.07)	$.63
Extraordinary credit	—	.05
Net (loss) income	$(.07)	$.68

statement of income

	Years ended July 31	
	1977	1976
Net sales (Note A)	$1,312,527	$1,201,002
Cost of sales (Note A)		
Beginning inventories	199,450	221,547
Purchases	582,563	443,042
Labor and overhead	451,842	464,384
Less ending inventories	(172,973)	(199,450)
	1,060,882	929,523
Gross profit from sales	251,645	271,479
Operating expenses		
Selling, general and administrative	138,219	163,473
Interest	52,431	55,789
	190,650	219,262
Income before Federal income tax	60,995	52,217
Provision for Federal income tax (Notes A and D)	21,856	23,134
Net income	$ 39,139	$ 29,083
Net income per common share (Note E)	$ .12	

paid for. But the expense occurred when the machine was depreciated or the raw materials were converted into finished widgets and sold.

This very important difference between an expenditure and an expense will become clearer as we go along. Let's continue with the Acme transactions in the first month of operations.

5. Space is rented and $250 is paid in advance for the first month's rent. Then on the last day of the month another $250 is paid for the next month's rent. Only the first $250 paid for the month of operations covered by this income statement will appear as an expense on the income statement. (The other $250 is "stored" in the balance sheet as a prepaid expense. It will become an expense against income after another month of operations.)

6. Salaries are paid to the owner-managers. The first month's total salary is $2,000. It won't be paid until several days into the second month. Even though it is not paid—no expenditure has been made—it will be recorded as an expense of the first month's operation.

7. During the first month, 1,200 widgets are manufactured and 1,000 are sold for $2.00 each. The customer has not yet paid for them when the month ends. The income statement will show sales of $2,000. It will show an expense for the widgets sold of $1,000 (each widget costs $1.00 in raw materials). The expense will not be $1,200. The extra $200 worth of widgets we manufactured are stored on the balance sheet in inventory. It will be an expense when the widgets are sold. The only expense for this month is the cost of the widgets we actually sold during the month.

These are enough transactions to allow us to construct an income statement.

Sales are $2,000. Expenses are $1,000 for the widgets we sold, $250 for rent, and $2,000 for salaries. Total expenses are $3,250. Since they exceed the amount of sales, we have no profit and therefore owe no taxes. Our bottom line shows a loss of $1,250. In the simple income statement format, it would look like this:

Sales	$2,000
Expenses	3,250
Taxes	-0-
Net Profit	(1,250)

One thing should be very clear from this exercise. Many important transactions are only partially shown or are not shown at all on the income statement. It sounds simple to say that the income statement shows sales, expenses, taxes, and profits, but the actual construction of an income statement is not so simple.

The income statement shows the sales made to customers during the period covered by the income statement. It shows the expenses incurred during the period—expenses that are associated with those sales or with operations during the period. It does *not* show money received for sales made in previous periods. It does *not* show expenditures made during the period that are not related to sales or operations for the period. It *does* show as expenses items that will actually be paid for later on.

The time frame within which the income statement operates is a very important concept. Every income statement—whether for a day, a month, or a year—has a specific beginning and ending. This income statement for that period shows the sales that were made during that period. More important and more difficult to grasp, it shows only those expenses that are associated with the sales made during the period or that are associated with activities going on during the period. When expenditures are made—before or after the specific period—is not reflected on the income statement.

Let's go on. Most income statements have more than the four categories we have discussed. A more common income statement format would look like this:

Items on Statement	Arithmetic Involved
Sales	*Sales* minus
Cost of Sales	*Cost of Sales* equals
Gross Profit	*Gross Profit* minus
Operating Expenses	*Operating Expenses* equals
Operating Profit	*Operating Profit* minus
Income Taxes	*Income Taxes* equals
Net Profit After Taxes	*Net Profit After Taxes*

The sales figure does not necessarily represent cash received by the company. The sales are what has been billed to customers (except in cash sales businesses). In most companies, all or part of the sales are in accounts receivable for some period of time.

The sales shown may not be real in another way. Customers may return their purchases in the next accounting period. These returns will reduce sales in that period. (Some companies set up reserves for returns, but this is not common.) To the extent that the sales figure is going to be reduced by future returns, it is overstated.

Sales may have been made to customers who won't pay. Are these real sales? They are reported like real sales, but perhaps they are something else. Sales figures are not always what they seem.

Expenses are not always what they seem either. We have already discussed the difference between the timing of expenditures and the recording of expenses. Depreciation is a particularly important example of an expense involving no direct cash outlay. (The cash has already been spent.) Other examples are setting up reserves or allowances, writing down assets, and similar transactions. As you remember from the balance sheet, these transactions decrease assets and correspondingly decrease retained earnings (or profits) even though no money changes hands when this kind of transaction is recorded.

Profits are also not cash. Items like depreciation and write-downs reduce profits but not current cash. Items that are accrued, such as salaries and taxes, reduce profits, but cash is normally not paid until a later period. The income statement may show good sales and good profits. But if the customers have not paid for the sales, the profits are not cash.

ACME WIDGET'S FIRST-YEAR INCOME STATEMENT

Let's construct an income statement for Acme Widget's first year of operations. The data we need to do this has already been compiled. You will find it in your balance sheet worksheet for year one. (Or use my worksheet in the Appendix.)

First, let's determine what the sales are for this period. Look through the worksheet until you find the transaction that shows this. My worksheet shows this as transaction number 11—sell $73,000 worth of widgets. So the first year's sales are $73,000.

Now we must come up with the cost of sales. This is the cost of the items that were sold during the period. The worksheet shows that we manufactured 41,000 widgets during the year. We purchased enough raw materials for 45,000 widgets. Neither of these items tells us what the cost of sales is.

What is important is that we sold 36,500 widgets. Therefore, the cost of sales will be the cost of the 36,500 widgets that were sold during the first year.

What is the cost of the 36,500 widgets we sold? Well, the raw materials in those widgets cost $1.00 each. At least part of the cost of sales would be the $36,500 of raw materials in the widgets we sold.

What about the cost of the widget machine? The expense for the first year is not the $12,000 we paid for the machine. It is the $1,200 in depreciation. The depreciation expense is the cost of using the machine during this period—its theoretical loss in value due to use, wear and tear, aging, and so forth during this period. The depreciation expense of $1,200 might be considered in the cost of sales.

But not the whole amount. The machine was used to manufacture 41,000 widgets and we only sold 36,500. 36,-500 is about 89 percent of 41,000. The cost of sales for this period should only include about 89 percent of the depreciation charge of $1,200. This is about $1,068. What happens to the other $132?

This would be stored in the cost of finished goods in inventory. The cost of the finished goods in inventory would be increased by the $132. When those goods were sold, that cost would become a cost of sales for that period.

In order to simplify things, we did not do things this way on the balance sheet exercises. We will ignore depreciation on this initial income statement exercise, too.

There is no end to the complications to cost of sales. Obviously the widget machine occupied space that was rented. So a portion of the rent should be charged to the cost of manufacturing the widgets. This cost would also go into inventory. The cost would move into cost of sales when the widgets were sold.

Someone had to operate the widget machine. The operator's salary should also be included as a cost of making the widgets. And so on. Accountants have developed various ways of determining when to stop assigning expenditures to the cost of sales. These tend to be arbitrary. Find out the system that is used in the company you are concerned with.

There is even a special branch of accounting that focuses closely on the allocation of costs to units of production. It is called cost accounting. We will not cover cost accounting in this book. If you are in a manufacturing business of any size, you will probably get involved in cost accounting. Get one of the many books on this topic or consult with your own cost accounting people.

For our purposes, we will be especially arbitrary and only assign the cost of the raw materials to the cost of sales of the widgets we sold.

The first-year cost of sales will then be $36,500.

The gross profit can be easily calculated. It is sales minus cost of sales. In Acme's first year, it is $73,000 minus $36,500. This equals a gross profit of $36,500.

Now let's get the operating expenses for the first year. Since we did not put depreciation into the cost of sales, we will treat it as an operating expense during this period.

Go through your worksheet and identify the other transactions which need to be recorded as expenses for this period of operations. I come up with rent, salaries, office expenses, and advertising. The total of operating expenses is $31,300 according to my calculations. What do you come up with?

Did all of these expenses involve cash outlays during the period? Of the $31,300 in expenses, how much actual cash was spent during the year?

Now let's calculate the operating profit. This is gross profit minus operating expenses. $36,500 minus $31,300 equals an operating profit of $5,200.

Our effective tax rate on this low income was set at 22 percent, and we came up with $1,150 owed in income taxes. Of course, we won't pay these taxes until several months after the end of the year.

The net profit after taxes is the operating profit minus income taxes. $5,200 minus $1,150 equals net profit after taxes of $4,050.

We can check back to see if that figure is correct. Look at the first-year balance sheet. What are the retained earnings? We have said that retained earnings are the net profit after taxes minus any dividends paid. We paid no dividends. So the retained earnings for the first year ought to

THE INCOME STATEMENT 83

be the same as the net profit after taxes for the first year. Are they?

Let's put the Acme Widget first-year income statement into a proper format. (See Figure 6 on the next page.)

MORE ON COST OF SALES

Cost of sales is complicated. Some companies don't even have it on their income statement. Not because it is too complicated, but because what they sell has no identifiable unit cost.

Companies that sell personal service—accounting firms, consulting companies, research labs, medical clinics, and so forth—have no real cost of sales. They have sales and expenses.

Figure 6

ACME WIDGET COMPANY
Income Statement for Year One

Sales	$73,000	100.0% of sales
Cost of Sales	36,500	50.0%
Gross Profit	36,500	50.0%
Operating Expenses	31,300	42.9%
Operating Profit	5,200	7.1%
Income Taxes	1,150	1.6%
Net Profit After Taxes	4,050	5.5%

Other kinds of companies also have little or no cost of sales. In an indoor tennis club, the product being sold is time on the courts. The construction cost of the courts is depreciated. There are expenditures for lighting, heat, maintenance, and so on. But these costs are normally not considered as costs of sales. Most indoor tennis clubs only show a cost of sale for their food and beverage operations and for their pro shops. The sale of court time has no cost of sales.

Golf clubs, ski areas, campgrounds, and many other kinds of recreational facilities whose main "product" is time at the facility do not normally show any cost of sales for the sales of time. The income statement would show sales and then operating expenses.

Many kinds of companies buy finished goods to sell. Wholesale and retail companies normally purchase finished products. It is relatively easy for them to calculate the cost of sales. It is the cost of the finished products that have been sold during the period. (Is the cost of transporting the finished product from the manufacturer to the company a cost of sales? It is often treated as a cost of sales. But some companies call this transportation cost an operating expense.)

In companies that manufacture their own products to sell, computing the cost of sales is more difficult. The raw materials, the depreciation of the machinery, the salaries of the workers who run the machines and handle the products through production, the cost of the space occupied in production, and so forth is allocated to each unit produced. Then when the unit is sold, the costs attached to that unit go out of inventory and into cost of sales.

A flow chart may help to make this somewhat less murky.

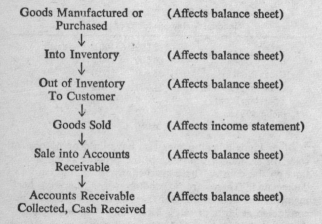

Goods Manufactured or Purchased	(Affects balance sheet)
Into Inventory	(Affects balance sheet)
Out of Inventory To Customer	(Affects balance sheet)
Goods Sold	(Affects income statement)
Sale into Accounts Receivable	(Affects balance sheet)
Accounts Receivable Collected, Cash Received	(Affects balance sheet)

You can see that the income statment is only affected at one point on this flow chart.

In many companies it is not practical to keep track of each individual unit that is flowing through. Cost of sales is computed from this formula:

Beginning Inventory *plus*
Purchases *equals*
Total Inventory Available *minus*
Ending Inventory *equals*
Cost of Sales

Let's apply this formula to Acme Widget. The beginning inventory was zero. Purchases during the year were $45,000 of raw materials. (Again we are simplifying by only considering raw materials.) Thus total inventory available was $45,000. The ending inventory (see the year one balance sheet) was $8,500. Subtract that from the total inventory available. Does the resulting figure give you the cost of sales that is shown on the year one income statement?

This is a very useful formula. Let's put it into algebraic form and then see what else we can do with it.

Let   B = Beginning Inventory
      P = Purchases
      E = Ending Inventory
      C = Cost of Sales

The formula is then:

$$B + P - E = C$$

This formula can then be solved for any unknown. If you know any three of the numbers, you can easily calculate the fourth.

Suppose you want to know how many dollars of purchases were made during the period. Your balance sheet shows the beginning inventory and the ending inventory. The income statement shows the cost of sales. You know three of the numbers in the formula. Now you can easily figure out the amount of purchases.

Suppose your boss says, "Don't let the ending inventory be any more than the beginning inventory." How much can you spend on purchases? Well, you already know two of the figures. Beginning inventory and ending inventory are going to be the same. It is obvious from the formula that your purchases must be exactly the same as your cost of sales.

What do you do if you want to reduce your ending inventory? Look at the formula. I find it useful to change it around so that $B + P - E = C$ becomes $B + P - C = E$. Then I can focus on the quantity that concerns me. In this case, ending inventory. To reduce ending inventory it is necessary to reduce purchases or to increase cost of sales. Or do both. The cost of sales can only be increased by increasing sales. To reduce inventory, sell more, purchase less, or do both. The formula will help you to see these relationships and to plan on what must be done to accomplish desired results.

This formula is a useful tool in planning, budgeting, and analysis.

NON-OPERATING INCOME AND EXPENSE

Most income statements add another entry. Sometimes it is two entries—non-operating income and non-operating expense.

Not all income or expense comes as a result of the regular operations of a company. Such non-operating income or expense is entered below the Operating Profit and prior to Income Taxes on the income statement.

What are some examples of these non-operating items? If a company has excess space, it may rent out some of it. If the company is not in the regular business of renting space, the rental income would be non-operating income.

Anytime a company pays interest on borrowed money, this is a non-operating expense. If a company earns interest by investing cash it doesn't need for operations in marketable securities, the interest earned is non-operating income.

Significant entries in either the non-operating income or expense area need to be investigated and analyzed. They may indicate problems.

Sometimes income statements show an entry below the operating profit labelled Extraordinary Item, or a similar title. Dive for the footnotes as soon as you see such an entry. The footnotes should explain what it is.

An extraordinary gain often results from a company selling off assets—disposing of a division, selling land or buildings or other fixed assets. If the extraordinary item is a loss, it is often the result of closing down a losing operation and recognizing all the bad receivables, bad inventory, and other overvalued assets that must be written down or written off.

ACME WIDGET'S SECOND-YEAR INCOME STATEMENT

Now it is time to construct the income statement for the second year of Acme's operations. This will be a comparative income statement. We will compare year one with year two. We will also calculate the percentages of sales for the various items to assist in analysis. Use the format on the next page.

Go back to the balance sheet worksheet for year two. Use your own or the one in the Appendix. This worksheet will show all of the transactions that affect the income statement.

It will also show a number of transactions that only affect the balance sheet. As the first step in preparing the income statement, prepare an income statement worksheet.

Your income statement worksheet should contain each of the headings that will appear on the income statement. Now go through the balance sheet worksheet. Look at each entry. Decide whether or not it affects the income statement or only the balance sheet.

ACME WIDGET COMPANY
Comparative Income Statement for Year Two

Item	Year Two	Percentage of Sales	Year One	Percentage of Sales
Sales				
Cost of Sales				
Gross Profit				
Salaries				
Advertising				
Machinery Depreciation				
Furniture and Fixtures				
Building Space Costs				
Other				
Total Operating Expenses				
Operating Profit				
Non-Operating Income and Expense				
Income Taxes				
Net Profit After Taxes				

If the entry affects the income statement, put in the entry that you will make under the appropriate heading on your worksheet. When you have finished, you can add up the entries under each heading. Then transfer the totals to the income statement.

For the second year, we will continue using the cost of the widget raw materials in cost of sales. We will not consider the machine operator's salary, the rental of the space occupied by the widget machine, machine depreciation, and other costs as part of the cost of sales. We will treat these expenditures as operating expenses. (Be careful. In the second year, the cost of sales must include some entries other than just the cost of the raw materials used in making the widgets that are sold.)

To calculate the Acme Widget cost of sales, use the formula, $B + P - E = C$.

When you use this formula, it should be clear to you what other entries will go into cost of sales in addition to the cost of the raw materials needed to manufacture the widgets sold.

Go to it.

The net profit after taxes of Acme Widget's second year of operations is $22,850. If that is not the answer you got, go back over your figures again. You have made a mistake. Dig until you find it.

When you feel confident you have everything just right, you can check your income statement against mine. See the Appendix.

RECONCILIATION OF RETAINED EARNINGS

Beneath many income statements is a section entitled Reconciliation of Retained Earnings. The purpose of this section is to tie the income statement and the balance sheet together. Sometimes the information is shown in a separate Statement of Retained Earnings. For Acme Widget the reconciliation of retained earnings for year one and two is shown on the next page.

This statement is self-explanatory. The net profit after taxes for the current period is added to the retained earnings at the end of the previous period. Any dividends paid during the current period are subtracted. What remains are the retained earnings at the end of the year. The number on this statement had better be the same number shown on the balance sheet or there is a big problem somewhere.

Reconciliation of Retained Earnings

Item	Year Two	Year One
Retained Earnings at Beginning of Year	$ 4,050	–0–
add Net Profit After Taxes	22,850	4,050
subtract Dividends Paid	3,000	–0–
Retained Earnings at End of Year	23,900	4,050

ANALYSIS OF INCOME STATEMENTS

There are several ways to analyze the component parts of an income statement.

1. Comparison with previous period—dollar comparison: This analysis method looks at the dollars and compares. Look at the comparative income statement for Acme Widget. (Use your own or the one in the Appendix.) You can see that sales increased by $77,000, operating expenses increased by $9,600, net profit after taxes increased by $18,800, and so on.
2. Comparison with previous period—percent comparison: The Acme Widget comparative income statement shows what percentage of sales each item is. For example, gross profit in year one was 50.0% of sales. In year two it declined to 49.2% of sales.
3. Percent change from previous period: Acme Widget sales went up by 105.5% from year one to year two. At the same time salaries went up by 35.0.%

No one method is necessarily best in all circumstances. You will want to try different methods of analysis to find out what is most meaningful to you in the particular circumstances.

In general, I find that looking at the dollar increase or percent increase (or decrease) is most useful for sales. Then the other items can be looked at as a percentage of sales. As sales increase it is desirable that many items represent a smaller percentage of sales. This is because many costs are relatively fixed. As sales increase, the costs won't increase, or they will increase at a much slower rate.

When cost of sales or operating expense items increase at a faster rate than the increase in sales, something is usually wrong. It is likely that too much is being spent to generate the additional sales. Trouble is on the horizon.

Another factor in analysis is deciding what previous period to compare with. If the income statement is for one month, it can be compared with the previous month. Or it can be compared with the same month in the previous year.

In businesses with a consistent and even pattern of operations, comparison with the previous period may be satisfactory. For seasonal businesses, make comparisons with the same period in the previous year. It would not make sense to compare the December sales of Christmas trees with the November sales. It is meaningful to compare this December with last December, assuming conditions are similar.

Comparisons can be made against averages of several previous periods—say, against the average for the past five years. Other standards can be chosen against which to make comparisons for purposes of analysis.

I strongly believe in comparing actual results with planned results. How well did you do compared with what you planned to do?

Actual vs. budget is probably the most useful comparison. It is especially helpful in analyzing operations. If things have not turned out as planned, what went wrong? What can be done about it? Perhaps plans need to be changed to take into account changed circumstances. Or perhaps operations must be altered to get in line with the plan. Having a plan is a very important aspect of business success. Comparing actual operations with the plan is a very important method of identifying business problems.

Look at the income statements that were shown at the beginning of this chapter. Get out your calculator so that you can figure out percentage change, items as a percent of sales, and so forth. What good trends or indications do you see? What warning signals do you see? What areas would you especially watch in future income statements?

COMPLICATING COST OF SALES

The Acme Widget operations for year two contain a number of complications in computing cost of sales. We used only the cost of the raw materials in the widgets to compute cost of sales. This is simple. It is also wrong.

The $8,400 we paid a worker to run the widget machine ought to be considered in cost of sales, too. But wait. The widget machine operator made 76,500 widgets and we only sold 75,000. We can't charge the entire salary to cost of sales.

Let's divide the machine operator's salary by the number of widgets manufactured. $8,400 ÷ 76,500 = $0.1098. The salary cost per widget was not quite eleven cents. The cost of sales of 75,000 widgets should contain a cost of 75,000 × $0.1098 = $8,235.

The cost of sales would now be $75,000 for the raw materials (at $1.00 of raw materials for each widget) plus $8,235 for a total of $83,235.

The machine operator's salary was $8,400. Cost of sales only includes $8,235. What happens to the other $165?

This salary expenditure is tied to the additional widgets that were manufactured but not sold. These 1,500 widgets went into the inventory. We expect to sell them in future periods. Included in the inventory are the raw materials in these widgets and the salary cost assigned to each one. Thus $165 in salary is stored in the inventory. It will come to the income statement as a cost of sales in some future period when those widgets come out of inventory and are sold.

In our year two income statement we showed the entire $8,400 salary of the machine operator as an operating expense. Now we have removed the $8,400 from operating expense. This will increase profits.

We put $8,235 additional into cost of sales. This will reduce profits. But notice. The $165 that is stored in inventory does not appear on the income statement. This makes our profits higher by $165 than they would have been under the original way we computed them.

If you want to make investors think your company is making good profits, it may be very nice to increase profits by $165.

But you have to pay taxes on the increased profit. So you may not be quite so happy about showing increased profits when you realize that it will result in your owing more taxes. In year two, Acme Widget paid 27.8 percent of its net profit before taxes in income taxes. An additional income of $165 will result in additional taxes of about $46 being owed.

You have paid the entire $8,400 in salary. These changes in cost of sales on the income statement do not affect what actually happened to the cash that came in or went out. But by resulting in more profit, it means that you will have to pay out more cash as taxes.

You can see that the way we compute the cost of sales has an important impact—not just on the score but also on real dollars.

There are further complications. The depreciation of $1,200 on the widget machine is surely associated with the manufacture of goods for sale. It, too, can be divided by the 76,500 widgets manufactured. $1,176 will appear in the cost of sales as the depreciation cost assigned to the 75,000 widgets sold. The remaining $24 will be assigned to widgets in inventory.

Year two profits will increase by $24 as a result of this. And additional income tax will be owed.

What about the space occupied by the raw materials, the machine, and the finished goods? Shouldn't rent or building depreciation also be assigned to widgets and either go into inventory or cost of sales?

In a large and complex manufacturing operation, a large number of various costs can be assigned to units, go into inventory, and then appear as cost of sales when the units are sold. Accountants and the IRS have general principles and regulations that help guide the assignment of costs.

Many managers want to minimize their tax liability. They want to have as many costs show up as current expenses as possible. They don't want costs stored away in inventory when they have already paid for the costs.

Some managers try to store as much cost as possible in inventory so that profits will be large and impressive. The desires of these different managers are tempered by what their auditors and the tax authorities will allow. In any case, all insist upon consistency. Whatever policies are followed should be followed consistently. It is impossible to analyze income statements or balance sheets if they do not follow consistent methods of handling transactions.

A chart may help to clarify some of the complications of the flow of cost of sales.

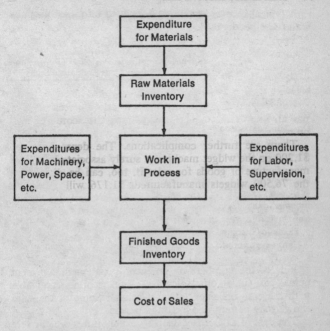

Only the cost of sales appears on the income statement. All of the transactions and activities which are shown above cost of sales in the chart affect the balance sheet.

SUMMARY OF THE INCOME STATEMENT

It is now time to summarize what has been presented on the income statement. This section has been considerably shorter than the one on the balance sheet. Yet most managers spend almost all of their time looking at income statements—budgeted or actual.

You have seen that many transactions affect the balance sheet but do not appear on the income statement until later—perhaps much later. Exclusive attention to the income statement may not be wise.

The income statement (or profit and loss statement, operating statement, statement of earnings, or other) summarizes the results of a company's operations over a period of time—usually a month, a quarter, or a year.

A typical income statement is divided into these sections with these headings.

Item	Current Period	Percentage of Sales	Previous Period or Budget	Percentage of Sales
Sales				
Cost of Sales				
Gross Profit				
Operating Expenses				
Operating Profit				
Non-Operating Income and Expense				
Net Profit Before Taxes				
Income Taxes				
Net Profit After Taxes (or Income, Earnings, or other)				

Few of the numbers on an income statement represent actual cash in or out. Sales are often accounts receivable with the cash collected later (if at all). Some of the sales shown may be returned in future periods.

The cost of sales reflects many expenditures which were made earlier when goods were purchased or manufactured. Many other purchases will not be paid for until later.

Some operating expenses are prepaid expenses where the cash went out in a previous period. Many operating expenses are represented by accounts payable or accruals. The actual cash will go out later when the expense is shown on the income statement.

Income taxes are usually payable later. Certainly the net profit after taxes is not spendable cash.

The sales shown on an income statement are those sales that are recorded during the accounting period, less any returns or sales adjustments.

The cost of sales (or cost of goods sold) includes all those costs directly associated with the items that were sold. Which actual costs are included in the cost of sales is a complex matter. Judgment is involved. Consistency is essential.

Expenditures for goods to be sold are first recorded in

the inventory on the balance sheet. Then they move out of the inventory into the cost of sales at the time a sale is made.

Cost of sales for companies with large inventories of many items can be calculated by the formula:

$$B + P - E = C$$

where   B = Beginning inventory
         P = Purchases
         E = Ending inventory
         C = Cost of sales

This formula can be used to arrive at purchases or inventory status as well as cost of sales.

Companies that sell personal services or time at their facilities often have no cost of sales on their income statements.

Operating expenses include all the expenses incurred to operate the business during the period. Some of these are non-cash expenses like depreciation or write-offs. Others are prepaid expenses, such as rent paid in advance. Still other operating expenses will result in future expenditures, such as salaries or purchases to be paid for in the future.

Non-operating income results from revenues that are not associated with a company's normal operations. (For example, interest earned on investments of idle cash.)

Non-operating expenses result from expenditures not associated with a company's normal operations. (Interest paid on borrowed money, for example.)

Income taxes are due on the net profit before taxes. Net profit and the income taxes due on the profit can be increased or decreased by the way in which various transactions are handled on the balance sheet and income statement.

Net profit after taxes (or whatever it is called) is the bottom line. It is a score, perhaps the most important score of all in the business game. At least it is the score that is most often referred to. But it is only a score. It does not represent spendable cash. The actual cash available may be much more or much less than the bottom-line profit figure shows.

Financial reports usually contain a reconciliation or statement of retained earnings. This shows how retained earnings at the beginning of the year have been increased during the year by net profit after taxes, and decreased by dividends paid. The retained earnings shown for the end of the year are the same as the figure shown in retained earnings on the balance sheet.

Income statements are usually analyzed by comparing figures for the current period with budgeted figures or with figures from a comparable previous period. Comparisons can be made in terms of dollars or percentage changes, or by looking at various items as a percent of sales.

The income statement is the primary format for budgeting. The income statement, or portions of it, most often is sent to managers of departments, divisions, and other subunits of companies. It is important to understand how an income statement is put together. It is important to understand what it shows and what it does not show. If you are still not clear about aspects of the income statement, skim through this chapter again. Practice with income statements available from other sources. Experience and practice will enable you to deal confidently and successfully with income statements.

7. Return on Investment (ROI)

THERE ARE many ways of measuring the success of a company. The contribution a company makes to society or human progress is one measure of success or failure. Another measure is the satisfaction and happiness of a company's customers or employees.

But in business the score is kept in dollars. We are concerned here with financial measures of success or failure. A company that serves society, satisfies its customers, and makes its employees happy—and loses money—will soon be out of business. The best kind of company is one that can do good in the world at the same time it makes money.

The simplest measure of financial success is the bottom line—net profit after taxes. A company with large net profits after taxes is successful. A company with a loss is a failure. This is straightforward but too simple.

Long ago, managers and investors began to question this simple bottom-line approach. "What if," they said, "Company A has an investment of $1 million and Company B has an investment of $2 million, and both companies produce the same net profit after taxes? Are they equally successful?"

The answer was "no." Company B had to have twice as much investment to produce the same profit or return as Company A. Therefore, it is much less successful than Company A.

The concept of return on investment was developed. Companies and their managers came to be measured by how much profit they could generate in relation to the investment they had to work with.

Another important consideration made return on investment a valuable measure.

If an investor could put his funds in safe U. S. government bonds, he would have a return on these funds and almost no risk of loss. If the investor were to put these funds into a business with risk, he would naturally expect to get a higher return. The higher the risk of loss, the higher the return the investor would expect. Return on investment thus became a method of comparing alternative uses of money.

The investors in Acme Widget put $30,000 into the company. At current interest rates, they could earn about $1,500 a year from very safe government bonds. They could get a return of perhaps $2,400 a year from the bonds of large, well-established companies. Presumably, the investors in Acme expect to do better than this. A new company, especially in the widget industry, can be a risky venture. The possibility that everything will be lost is significant. Because of the risk of loss, the possibility of return must be high.

There is another factor that favors measurement by return on investment. When all of the attention is focused on the bottom line of the income statement, a company can get into serious trouble. Remember, profits aren't cash. But it can take a lot of cash to buy inventory and fixed assets. If customers pay slowly, a lot of cash can be tied up in accounts receivable. Assets can soak up all available cash—and more—while a company's net profit after taxes looks great. Then one day the company can't pay its bills, and it goes bankrupt or is taken over by someone else.

So managers must control the investment at the same time they work to produce profits. Return on investment measurements help to keep everybody looking at both profits and investment.

There are a number of different ways of computing return on investment (ROI). We will discuss five main ones.

1. Return on Equity (ROE).
2. Return on Invested Capital (ROIC).
3. Return on Assets Used (ROAU).
4. Cash-on-Cash Return.
5. Discounted Cash Flow or Present Value Method.

The figures below repeat the key numbers from the Acme Widget financial reports that will be needed to compute return on investment.

Balance Sheet

Assets	Year Two	Year One
Cash and Marketable Securities	$ 8,710	$ 650
Other Current Assets	48,300	25,750
Non-Current Assets	41,240	10,800
Liabilities		
Current Liabilities	24,350	13,150
Long-Term Liabilities	20,000	-0-
Capital	53,900	24,050

Income Statement

Operating Profit	$32,900	$ 5,200
Non-Operating Expense	900	-0-
Net Profit After Taxes	22,850	4,050

RETURN ON EQUITY (ROE)

Return on Equity shows the amount of profits as a percent of the owner's investment, net worth, or equity. Return in the ROE formula is net profit after taxes. Equity is net worth or total capital. The formula is:

$$\text{ROE} = \frac{\text{Net Profit After Taxes}}{\text{Equity}}$$

A complication with this and other return on investment formulas must be resolved. When is the investment measured? Is it the investment at the beginning of the accounting period? The investment at the end of the period? Or the average investment during the period? Each of these choices has somewhat different consequences. In relatively stable situations it really does not matter which is used as long as comparisons are made on a consistent basis. For the examples in this chapter we will use the investment at year-end.

Acme Widget Return on Equity:

$$\text{Year One ROE} = \frac{4,050}{24,050} = .1684 = 16.8\%.$$

$$\text{Year Two ROE} = \frac{22,850}{53,900} = .4239 = 42.4\%.$$

Recent industry figures show that the average ROE runs about 12 percent. You can see that Acme Widget looks like a very good business. (I apologize for having such a high return. When I began constructing the Acme Widget example some chapters back, I did not plan ahead to the return on investment chapter. I would be much happier if these examples were more in the normal business range. But you will at least see how the return on investment is calculated even if the results are hardly typical of industry in general.)

Return on Equity is a good measure of company performance when most of the investment in the company is in the form of equity or when the analysis is being made for the owners.

RETURN ON INVESTED CAPITAL (ROIC)

Return on invested capital shows the return on the total investment in a company. Return in the ROIC formula is net profit after taxes plus interest paid on long-term debt. Investment is the equity plus any long-term debt or liabilities. Since the interest paid on long-term debt is a return on that investment, it must be added back to net profit after taxes to get the total return on invested capital, which includes both equity and long-term debt. The formula is:

$$\text{ROIC} = \frac{\text{Net Profit After Taxes} + \text{Interest on Long-Term Debt}}{\text{Capital} + \text{Long-Term Debt}}$$

The Acme Widget return on invested capital works out like this.

$$\text{Year One ROIC} = \frac{4,050}{24,050} = .1684 = 16.8\%$$

(Since Acme Widget has no long-term debt in year one, the ROIC is exactly the same as ROE.)

$$\text{Year Two ROIC} = \frac{22,850 + 900}{53,900 + 20,000} = \frac{23,750}{73,900} = .3214 = 32.1\%$$

This measure gives a much lower return on investment for year two than does the return on equity measure. With average industry return on invested capital running about 9 percent, it again appears that Acme Widget is doing a fantastic job. (And the author, less than fantastic.)

In this measure of ROIC, the problem of timing of investment is more serious. Acme's beginning invested capital was $24,050. At mid-year the owners invested an additional $10,000 in capital and additional long-term debt of $20,000 was taken on. This made the ending invested capital $73,900. Average invested capital would be $48,975.

ROIC might be 98.8 percent or 48.5 percent or 32.1 percent, depending upon the time period chosen for invested capital measurement.

Return on invested capital is generally a more satisfactory method of analysis than return on equity. Most companies have some long-term liabilities. For many companies, this debt represents a major portion of the investment. ROIC gives a much more meaningful indication of how well the management is using its total resources to produce profit.

RETURN ON ASSETS USED (ROAU)

Return on assets used is most useful for measuring the performance of divisions of companies where the divisions have little or no control over liabilities or capital.

In most multi-division companies the corporate headquarters raises the funds and allocates them to the division. Corporate headquarters often decides when to pay off liabilities. The division cannot control all of its investment.

Since corporate headquarters is responsible for borrowing funds and paying the interest, and since income taxes are usually paid on the total corporate results rather than on a single division, the division cannot really control its net profit after taxes.

In the ROAU formula, return is operating profit. Investment includes all those assets used to generate a profit. In many corporations the corporate treasurer controls cash and marketable securities. So these are not included among the assets used by the division. The selection of what items to include in an ROAU formula is arbitrary. The basic principle is to include all profits directly attributable to the division and all assets which the division uses to produce its profits.

The general formula is:

$$ROAU = \frac{\text{Operating Profit}}{\text{Assets Used}}$$

Let's apply this formula to the Acme Widget Company. I don't include cash as an asset in my calculations.

$$\text{Year One ROAU} = \frac{5,200}{36,550} = .1423 = 14.2\%$$

$$\text{Year Two ROAU} = \frac{32,900}{89,540} = .3674 = 36.7\%$$

As you can see, the return on investment is quite different with different formulas. ROE gives a different figure than ROIC, which is different than ROAU. Any of the formulas can be useful. You will need to decide which is best for you in the particular circumstances. Then you must apply the formula consistently. Do it the same way for each year. The trend or changes from year to year will be the important information.

ROE, ROIC, and ROAU are methods usually used to analyze past performance. The methods which follow are usually used to analyze future possibilities.

CASH-ON-CASH RETURN

This method of analyzing results is typically used in real estate deals or anywhere else where cash return on cash investment is the important yardstick.

In calculating cash-on-cash return, the return is the cash actually generated by the operation. This may bear little relation to the profit reported.

The investment is the actual cash invested. Cash-on-cash return says "We put so many dollars of cash into this deal. How many dollars are we getting out?"

We will not calculate the cash-on-cash return for Acme Widget. You can do so if you wish. But you will run into a problem. What is the cash return? Is it the cash actually taken out of the business ($3,000 in dividends during year two)? Or is it the cash that might have been taken out if we wanted to strip all the cash out of the company?

Cash-on-cash return is not suited to analyzing an operation like Acme Widget or most other going businesses like this. It is much better for real estate operations where money flows out to the owners and is generally not retained in the business as working capital. When money is put into inventory, tied up in accounts receivable, and so forth, it is difficult to figure cash-on-cash return so that it means something.

Still, cash-on-cash return can be a good way to analyze potential investment opportunities. An investor does eventually expect to get cash back for the cash invested.

For example, Acme invested $1,500 to obtain a patent license. How much extra cash will be generated by this investment of $1,500? If the investment will result in a return of $70 a year (4.7 percent return on investment) it is probably better to put the money into a savings account.

On the other hand, if the cash return is going to be $300 a year (20 percent return on investment), it might be a good investment.

Cash-on-cash return can be used to compare alternative proposals or to evaluate future projects and opportunities.

PAYBACK METHOD

The payback method of analysis is not strictly a return on investment measurement. Nevertheless, this is as good a place as any to mention it.

The payback method asks how long it will take to get the money back that is invested in a project. The answer is usually given in years. If a project will pay back its investment in five years, it has a five-year payback. A five-year payback is better than a ten-year payback, all other things being equal.

DISCOUNTED CASH FLOW OR PRESENT VALUE METHOD

Comparing projects or evaluating future projects by the methods we have been discussing has two important problems.

1. Few projects, deals, or businesses have the same profit or return each year. Often money is lost in the early years. Then the breakeven point is reachd. After a period of time profits begin to come in. These profits often fluctuate up or down. This uneven return makes it hard to calculate a return on investment over a period of time. How does one balance loss years with profit years?

2. A dollar in hand today is worth more than a dollar available in the future. Inflation may reduce the value of

the future dollar. A dollar available today can be invested in a savings account, government securities, or elsewhere and earn a return each year. A dollar available five years in the future cannot earn any return for five years. How does one balance the value of present dollars against the value of future dollars?

The discounted cash flow or present value method of analysis was devised to deal with uneven flows of funds in and out and with the fact that dollars available in the future are worth less than dollars available now.

Let's see what one dollar invested at 5 percent interest, will be worth in five years.

Beginning of year 1 . . . $1.00.
End of year 1 . . . interest earned on $1.00 = $0.050.
    Total amount in hand . . . $1.050.
End of year 2 . . . interest earned on $1.050 = $0.0525.
    Total amount in hand . . . $1.1025.
End of year 3 . . . interest earned on $1.1025 = $0.0551.
    Total amount in hand . . . $1.1576.
End of year 4 . . . interest earned on $1.1576 = $0.0579.
    Total amount in hand . . . $1.2155.
End of year 5 . . . interest earned on $1.2155 = $0.0608.
    Total amount in hand . . . $1.2763.

At the end of five years, $1.00 will have grown to $1.28 (rounded off) at 5 percent interest compounded annually.

Therefore, a dollar in hand today is worth 28 cents more than a dollar available in five years, if we use the 5 percent rate of interest. At 10 percent compounded annually, a dollar today is worth 61 cents more than a dollar available in five years. At a 14 percent rate of interest a dollar can be doubled in five years.

In using the discounted cash flow or present value method, the question is usually turned around. It asks, "What will a dollar received in the future be worth today?"

Look at the table on the next page. This is a section of a table found in many accounting, and business mathematics, books. It is also reproduced in greater detail in the back of this book. It is called a present value table. It shows the present value of a dollar received at some future time.

Analysis by the present value method requires the use of a present value table (or a calculator that can compute present value).

Take a look at the present value table in the back of this book. You will see that it shows many interest rate percentages and many years.

Look at the table. Find the column headed 10 percent. Go down to the row for five years in the future. There you can see that at 10 percent interest, a dollar received five years in the future has a value of $0.6209 today. To put it another way, $0.6209 invested today at 10 percent interest compounded annually will grow to $1.00 after five years.

Present Value of $1

Years in the Future	5%	7%	10%	12%
1	.9524	.9346	.9091	.8929
2	.9070	.8734	.8264	.7972
3	.8638	.8163	.7513	.7118
4	.8227	.7629	.6830	.6355
5	.7835	.7130	.6209	.5674
10	.6139	.5083	.3855	.3220
20	.3769	.2584	.1486	.1037

We said before that a dollar in hand today would be $1.61 in five years at 10 percent. Let's check this out. Multiply $1.61 by the present value at the five year-10 percent intersection.

$1.61 × .6209 = $1.00 (allowing for rounding off error.)

Let's do some exercises with this table. If you are to get $1,000 in four years, what amount of money today would be its equivalent, if you invested in a 5 percent savings account?

(Formula: $1,000 × .8227 = ?)

Your business is making a cash-on-cash return of 12 percent. You can invest $8,000 in a special deal that will pay off in just two years. How much will the deal need to pay off to equal your usual 12 percent return?

(Formula: $8,000 × .7972 = ?)

Is this a good deal if you get back $9,600 after two years? After all, $9,600 is a gain of $1,600 on your investment of $8,000—a return on investment of 20 percent. Isn't this 20 percent return much better than the 12 percent you want? Not over two years. Let's demonstrate.

Beginning of year 1 . . . $8,000.
End of year 1 . . . Return of 12% on $8,000 = $960.
Total amount in hand at end of year 1 . . . $8,960.
End of year 2 . . . Return of 12% on $8,960 = $1,075.20.
Total amount in hand at end of year 2 . . . $10,035.20.
Total two-year gain is $2,035.20.

This is a return of better than 25 percent. You can see that it is better to get 12 percent a year compounded than the return of 20 percent after two years.

You will get more practice in using the present value table in examples below. The discounted cash flow or present value method uses the present value table to evaluate plans for the future. Here is one case.

Don Baker, owner of Midwest Widgets, comes to us. He would like to sell out his small company and retire. He asks if we are interested. We ask for some information. Then we make a projection.

Baker wants $81,000 for his company. He says he will take $24,000 down and the remainder over the next three years—three annual installments paid at year-end, with interest of 7 percent on the unpaid balance. We would have to pay Baker the following:

Immediately	$24,000
End of first year	$19,000 plus interest of $3,990
End of second year	$19,000 plus interest of $2,660
End of third year	$19,000 plus interest of $1,330
Principal of	$81,000 plus interest of $7,980

Total payment over three years would be $88,980.

Midwest Widgets has been making money. Last year's net profit after taxes was $11,000. The business has been stable over the past several years.

When Baker retires, his salary of $21,000 a year will end. But we will need to hire an assistant to handle the extra business that the merger to Midwest into Acme will bring. We expect to pay $12,000 a year to the assistant. So we save $9,000 a year in salary costs, before taxes.

With our better production control and selling effort we expect to increase sales with little increase in expenses. So the acquisition of Midwest will add to the Acme profits. Our best guess is that the additional net profit after taxes will be as follows:

First year	$ 16,000
Second Year	$ 19,000
Third year	$ 21,000
Fourth year	$ 23,000
Fifth year	$ 24,000
Five-year Total	$103,000

Over five years we will have paid $88,980 to acquire Midwest Widgets, and we will have made a return of $103,000. The return will be $14,100 more than the investment. The return on investment will be 15.8 percent. Is it a good deal or not?

Let's see.

We will make a table which brings all of the investment and all of the return down to present value. This takes care of the fact that the investment and return are made over a period of time and at varying amounts. By reducing everything to its present value we eliminate the effect of timing differences.

We must make a decision. At what percent shall we calculate present value? This is a critical question. If you compare this deal with investing in a savings account at 5 percent interest, then present value should be computed at 5 percent.

As you know, Acme Widget has been making a very high return on investment. But we have decided to see if the Midwest Widgets deal is a good deal at a 10 percent rate. If it isn't any good at 10 percent, it won't be any good at a higher rate. If it is OK at 10 percent, then perhaps we will want to compute the present values at, say, the 15 percent rate. At some rate it will cease being a good deal. Let's set up the table based on 10 percent.

Here is the table we construct to analyze this deal by the present value method.

	INVESTMENT			RETURN		
End of Year	Amount	Present Value Factor	Present Value	Amount	Present Value Factor	Present Value
0	$24,000 ×	1.0000 =	$24,000.00	—	—	—
1	22,990 ×	.9091 =	20,900.21	$ 16,000 ×	.9091 =	$14,545.60
2	21,660 ×	.8264 =	17,899.82	19,000 ×	.8264 =	15,701.60
3	20,330 ×	.7513 =	15,273.93	21,000 ×	.7513 =	15,777.30
4	—	—	—	23,000 ×	.6830 =	15,709.00
5	—	—	—	24,000 ×	.6209 =	14,901.60
Total	$88,980		$78,073.96	$103,000		$76,635.10

The table has two sides—investment and return. (Or it might be cash put in/cash taken out, or some such.) The years are shown at the left. We start with zero because the $24,000 down payment is made at the very beginning. "1" means the end of year one, and so forth.

Under investment we show the actual amount paid for each period. Under return we show the actual amount received for each period. These actual amounts are multiplied by the present value factor. (Taken from the present value table—years one through five at 10 percent.) The result of this multiplication is the present value of each amount invested or returned.

When we add up the present values, we see that the total present value of the investment exceeds the total present value of the return—over a five-year period at 10 percent. This indicates that the deal proposed by Don Baker is not a good one.

To be a good deal—at 10 percent rate over five years—we need to reduce the amount we pay to Baker or increase the net profit after taxes we make. It is a reasonably simple matter to try different numbers to determine what would be a good deal.

Now this calculation is based on three critical assumptions:

1. The amount of return or net profit after taxes we can get each year. Our estimate or projection could be way off. We might sell a lot more or find more savings. But any assumption about future profits must be reasonable and conservative.
2. The length of time we are willing to consider for this deal. Five years is a very short time for a dam or nuclear power plant. It is a long time for a fashion or fad business. The number of years over which the present value is calculated must be reasonable and conservative.
3. The rate we will use to compute present value. If we had idle funds that could earn no better than 5 percent, then perhaps a 10 percent rate is too high. If we can earn 20 percent investing the money somewhere else, then a 10 percent rate is too low. The rate chosen must be reasonable. Different rates can be tried.

These assumptions about future profits, time, and rate must be carefully made. In our Don Baker–Acme Widget example, we could make this seem like a good deal or a bad deal by changing the assumptions.

1. If we assume less profits, the deal is lousy. If we assume more profits, the deal could be good.
2. If we consider the deal over ten years, it will be good for us. Over three years, it looks awful.
3. If we are satisfied to get 5 percent return, then this is a favorable deal. If we need 10 percent or more, then this deal won't be to our advantage.

Let's set up another problem. You can make your own assumptions, set up your own table, and calculate the present values to see if it is a good deal.

Acme Widget customers are asking for fluted widgets. This may be a fad, but the first inquiry came to us almost two years ago. Now a lot of customers are asking for them.

It takes a special machine to make fluted widgets. To

purchase a fluted widget machine will cost $18,000. The machine maker demands payment on delivery.

We will have to hire a widget machine operator to run the fluted widget machine. The operator will cost $9,000 a year in salary. We have space in which to put the machine without any increase in that cost. We will disregard the costs of power, maintenance, and so on.

Fluted widgets use $1.10 worth of raw materials. The machine can turn out 25,000 fluted widgets a year.

Our normal widgets sell for $2.00 each. Competitors' fluted widgets usually sell for $2.30 to $2.50 each. Our rough market research indicates that we might sell from 12,000 to 30,000 fluted widgets a year. Somewhere in between these extremes lie the likely sales.

Acme Widget has excess cash. This cash is currently invested in securities that pay interest of 6 percent. We will have to have the cash now invested in securities to buy the machine. Our regular widget business provides a much better return than 6 percent. Eventually, we may want to expand our regular widget business. If so, we will need more money to finance the growth of working capital. The fluted widget business may be an immediate business growth opportunity.

Should we go into the fluted widget business?

First you must make your assumptions.

1. Profit—How many widgets can you sell? At what price? When you figure this out, then subtract 55 cents for each widget sold to cover variable operating expenses—sales commissions, order fulfillment costs, shipping expense, and so forth.

2. Time—For how long a period will you do this analysis? Will fluted widgets be a long-term staple product or a short-term fad? How far into the future do you want to project? Pick a number of years.

3. Rate—What rate of return should be used? Is the 6 percent interest that Acme is getting from securities the right rate? Or is a higher rate, more consistent with Acme's high return on investment, more suitable? You must choose a rate.

When you have made these assumptions, then set up your table. Use a format like this:

FLUTED WIDGET DEAL

Year	Cash Paid Out			Cash Received		
	Amount	Present Value Factor	Present Value	Amount	Present Value Factor	Present Value
0						
1						
2						
3						
↓						
Total						

Enter the amounts into the table. For ease of computation, assume that all cash coming in or going out arrives or leaves at the beginning or ending of a year—even though we know that cash will be flowing in and out all year long.

When you have determined the present value of cash paid out and cash received, then determine whether or not you would recommend that Acme buy a fluted widget machine.

My answer can be found in the Appendix. Don't look at it until you have done your own computations. Your answer may be quite different from mine. That may be because your assumptions are quite different from mine. As long as you have used the correct method, your answer is as good as mine. All either of us can say is that based on our assumptions this is a good deal or a bad deal for Acme Widget.

This is a brief presentation of the discounted cash flow or present value method of analysis. There are whole books on this topic if you are interested. I have found that this amount of information is sufficient for almost all business needs.

One last word. You can see why this is called the present value method. All amounts are brought to their present value. Why is it also called the discounted cash flow method?

You can probably guess. The cash flow—in and out—is discounted or reduced in value if it occurs in the future. The amount that the cash flow is discounted is determined by the present value table.

SUMMARY

We began this chapter by discussing various methods of measuring return on investment. Return on investment isn't the only way to measure the success or value of a company. But it is a far better method than just looking at net profit.

Return on investment (ROI) measures the profit a company generates from the resources it has to work with. ROI is a measure that encourages managers to manage both profits (the income statement) and assets and liabilities (the balance sheet). Problems in either area can be signaled by ROI measures.

We discussed three main ROI measures:

1. Return on Equity (ROE) = $\dfrac{\text{Net Profit After Taxes}}{\text{Owner's Equity}}$

2. Return on Invested Capital (ROIC) =
$\dfrac{\text{Net Profit After Taxes} + \text{Interest on Long-Term Debt}}{\text{Capital} + \text{Long-Term Debt}}$

3. Return on Assets Used (ROAU) =
$\dfrac{\text{Operating Profit}}{\text{Assets Used to Produce Profit}}$

ROE is a good measure when the owners are concerned about the return on their own investment. ROIC is a good measure of the return generated by the total investment in a business. It is especially important to use ROIC when a company has a heavy debt as part of its long-term investment. ROAU is a good measure for divisions where liability management and cash control are in the hands of corporate headquarters.

Any ROI measure is relative. Different industries have different historical ROIs. The trend of ROI is usually more significant than the absolute percentage for a year.

We mentioned cash-on-cash return as a method for evaluating deals where cash going in vs. cash coming out is the crucial concern. Cash-on-cash return is especially suited for real estate deals or for deals where profits do not need to be re-invested in working capital growth.

The payback method is used principally to evaluate new projects. It asks, "How long will it take to get back the money we invest in this project?"

Because a dollar in hand today is worth more than a dollar received in the future, we discussed the discounted cash flow or present value method of analysis. Using this method to evaluate acquisitions, projects, purchases, or operations requires making three assumptions:

1. What will the results be? (Profit projection.)
2. Over how long a time do we measure? (Time frame.)
3. What rate of return are we satisfied to have? (Interest percent.)

With these three assumptions in hand, plus a present value table and a calculator, we can make a sophisticated measure of whether or not something is valuable or a good opportunity.

There are other methods of measurement and analysis. You can study further if you care to. The ones we have discussed will serve for most purposes. Let me stress this in closing the chapter: Any return on investment (ROI) method of analysis is superior to just looking at profits.

8. Changes in Financial Position

THE FINANCIAL REPORTS of public companies contain three main items—balance sheet, income statement, and statement of changes in financial position. The purpose of the statement of changes in financial position is to make clear the flow of funds into, through, and out of the company. In the past, this statement was often called a funds flow statement.

We have seen that the balance sheet and income statement do not show the flow of cash and other financial resources very well. It is not always easy to see where the funds came from. It is not always easy to see what they were used for. The statement of changes in financial position attempts to reveal this information.

Basically, this statement shows the changes from one balance sheet to the next. It is structured like this:

> Sources of financial resources *minus*
> Uses of financial resources *equals*
> Change in financial position.

Financial resources are defined as working capital. Working capital is the reservoir of funds circulated to produce operating profits. Funds are not just cash in the bank. Funds in working capital also include accounts receivable, inventory, and other current assets.

Think of working capital as a circulating reservoir. Inventory is acquired. When it is sold, the funds move from inventory to accounts receivable. When the accounts are collected, the funds move into cash. The cash is used to pay the supplier of the inventory. This reduces cash but also reduces accounts payable so that working capital remains the same.

The statement of changes in financial position first tells us if any financial resources have been added to the working capital reservoir—and where they came from. Was more water put into the reservoir (to use a liquid analogy)?

Then the statement tells if any financial resources were taken away from the working capital reservoir—and where they went. Was any water drained off the reservoir?

The statement of changes in financial position then tells us where the financial resources are located in the reservoir. What is the water level in each part of the reservoir?

The typical statement of changes in financial position uses this format or something like it:

Sources of financial resources or working capital:
Net profit after taxes.
Depreciation and other items not requiring the use of working capital during the period (sometimes referred to as non-cash expenses.)
Total from operations.

(These two items—net profit and non-cash expenses—provide financial resources from the internal operations of the company. To this are added other sources of financial resources or working capital.)

Sales of fixed assets or other non-current assets.
Stock issued.
Long-term borrowing.
Total sources of financial resources or working capital.

Uses or application of financial resources or working capital:
Purchase of fixed assets or other non-current assets.

(The use of financial resources to purchase current assets does not change working capital.)

Payment of dividends.
Reduction in long-term debt.
Purchase of stock.

(If a company buys back its own stock, it is using its financial resources to reduce outstanding capital.)

Total uses or application of financial resources or working capital.
Net change in working capital.

(Recall that sources minus uses equals change.)

Changes in working capital

(This heading is followed by an analysis of the increases and decreases in each item of current assets and current liabilities making up working capital.)

Sources of working capital are profits, sale of non-current assets, increases in long-term liabilities, and increases in capital. (Profits may be thought of as a form of increase in capital since they increase retained earnings.)

Uses of working capital are purchases of non-current assets, reductions in long-term liabilities, or reductions in capital (through payment of dividends or repurchase of stock.)

Let's turn to the balance sheet and income statement for Acme Widget. We will construct a statement of changes in financial position for year two. This will make things more clear.

Use the statement format that follows. Fill it in from your own reports or from those in the Appendix.

ACME WIDGET COMPANY
Statement of Changes in Financial Position

Year Two

Sources of working capital
    Net profit after taxes
    Depreciation
        Total from operations
    Stock issued
    Long-term borrowing
        Total sources of working capital
Uses of working capital
    Purchase of fixed assets
    Purchase of intangible asset
    Dividends paid
    Reduction in long-term debt
    Purchase of stock
        Total uses of working capital
Increase in working capital
Changes in working capital
    Cash and marketable securities
    Accounts receivable, net after reserve
    Inventory, net after write-down
    Prepaid expenses
    Accounts payable
    Accruals

Working capital at beginning of year
Working capital at end of year

The change in working capital should be $19,410. You can check your statement of changes in financial position for Acme Widget against the one in the Appendix. Go back over your figures if your statement does not agree with the version in the Appendix.

What does this statement tell us?

First, it shows that Acme got funds from profits, from issuing stock, and from borrowing. It shows how much from each source. This can all be deduced from the comparative balance sheet. But it is more clearly revealed here.

The statement shows that a substantial portion of the funds were used to purchase fixed assets—in this case, the building. Dividends were paid. Enough was left over to increase working capital.

The statement shows where the increase in working capital is located. The total increase in current assets was $30,610. Some of this was financed by an increase in current liabilities—$11,200. The rest came from sources outside of the working capital items—$19,410.

This statement of changes in financial position will help investors, analysts, and managers see more easily how funds flowed into, through, and out of the company during the year.

SUMMARY

The statement of changes in financial position focuses on working capital as the financial resource reservoir of the company. The statement shows sources of working capital—net profit and non-cash expenses (especially depreciation) from operations, sales of non-current assets, issuing of stock, and long-term borrowing.

The statement of changes in financial position shows the uses of working capital—to purchase non-current assets, to pay dividends, to repurchase stock, and to repay long-term debt. Sources minus uses equals change in working capital.

The statement then analyzes the changes in each item of current assets and current liabilities to detail how the change in working capital applied to the specific items.

The statement of changes in financial position is derived from the balance sheet and income statement. Its purpose is to clarify the flow of funds that brought about changes in the balance sheet.

This statement may be used in planning ahead. But it is not as useful as the cash flow budget, which we will discuss next.

9. Cash Flow Budget

ONE OF THE most useful management tools is the cash flow budget. Preparing this budget will force the manager to consider many facets of the operation. This budget draws upon information that affects the balance sheet, income statement, and other reports.

A cash flow statement can be prepared as another kind of financial report. It is not found in the financial reports issued by public companies. It would contain more detail than these companies would care to reveal. A cash flow statement would also probably not be of great use to investors and analysts. It is much more valuable as a management tool.

The statement of changes in financial position tells what happened to the company's financial resources. In the Acme Widget statement of changes in financial position for year two, we can see that the company increased its cash and marketable securities (almost cash) by $8,060. This may be enough historical information. It gives the score. But this information format is not helpful in planning ahead.

The cash flow budget is much more useful. Let's see exactly how.

We will look ahead to Acme Widget's third year. We want to see how the purchase of a fluted widget machine will affect our cash situation. (See Chapter 7.)

Making up the cash flow budget will require much thought about the operations. Estimates will need to be made. Plans will have to be formulated. This kind of thinking is what makes preparation of the cash flow budget such a valuable exercise.

I will do most of the estimating and projecting for this cash flow budget. But you will still find much to do. Here are the key estimates and projections for the Acme Widget third year:

1. Sales of regular widgets will increase to 82,500 units at $2.00 each—total sales of $165,000. Widget sales are fairly steady throughout the year. Approximately the same number of widgets will be sold each month. However, July and August are vacation months and sales drop to 80 percent of the average in these months. Sales in September and October, after the vacation season ends, increase to 120 percent of the monthly average.

2. We will order a fluted widget machine at the beginning of the year. It will be delivered in March. The supplier does not extend credit. We will need to pay $18,000 in cash on delivery.

3. On April 1 we will hire an operator for the fluted widget machine. The operator will be paid $750 per month ($9,000 annually.) Other salaries will continue as they were in year two. The monthly total for the old employees is $2,700. In December, we hope to be able to pay a Christmas bonus—$2,000 to be divided among the employees.

4. Office expenses of $50 per month continue throughout the year. We must pay $150 a month for interest on the mortgage.

5. We will spend $750 for advertising in the months of February, May, September, and November. An extra advertising expense of $1,000 will be spent in April to announce our fluted widgets.

6. Fluted widget sales will develop over time. The first two months we have the machine, no fluted widgets will be sold. The sales by month thereafter are estimated as follows:

Month	Widgets Sold × $2.30 each =	Dollar Sales
May	600	$ 1,380
June	800	1,840
July	1,000	2,300
August	1,100	2,530
September	1,400	3,220
October	1,500	3,450
November	1,600	3,680
December	1,600	3,680
	9,600 units	$22,080

7. We decide to try to hold ending inventory to about the level it is at the beginning of the year. To do this, we will need to buy the raw materials for each widget we sell—$1.00 for each regular widget and $1.10 for each fluted widget. In January, we pay the raw material supplier the amount we owe him at year-end. Thereafter we order on a monthly basis. The supplier gives us credit. On the average, we pay 30 days after we get our monthly order.

8. The tax bill of $9,150 will be due on April 15. In October we hope to pay our shareholders a dividend of ten cents a share ($3,000.)

9. The primary source of cash will be collections from our customers. Our average collection period has been over 70 days. We expect to reduce that to 60 days by vigorous collection efforts and by selling to certain poor accounts for cash only. At the beginning of year three, customers owe us $30,000, less the reserve of $1,500. These accounts represent sales over the last months of year two. We expect to collect 40 percent of these accounts receivable in January. Another 40 percent should be collected in February, and the remainder will be collected in March. We will begin collecting for the sales made in year three in March (60 days after the sales made in January.)

See the cash flow budget in Figure 7. I have prepared the budget for the first six months of year three. You should fill in the numbers of the last six months.

You recognize, of course, that this is a greatly simplified budget. We have ignored such important factors as inflation, increased costs due to the installation of the fluted widget machine, FICA and other employee benefits required by law, and much more. An actual cash flow budget can become quite complicated. (Or it can be simplified by lumping together many items whose effect upon the totals will be insignificant.)

Let's look at the cash flow budget for the first six months. It is clear that Acme has a cash flow problem in March and April. The payment for the fluted widget machine drains off all the cash. $2,470 more is needed to pay all the bills.

In April, collections fall off and taxes must be paid. $6,-925 more is needed to pay the bills this month.

Now you see the purpose of the cash flow budget. It

pinpoints cash flow problems. It allows the manager to plan on how to deal with the problems.

Acme has to come up with an additional $9,665 in cash to pay all its bills in March and April. It probably needs to have more cash than this. Some money ought to be in the bank as a cushion or emergency fund. Acme probably ought to get $11,000 or $12,000. How?

More stock can be issued. But a more likely source of cash is a bank. How long will Acme need to have this money? Can it all be paid back before the end of the year?

A banker would certainly want to know.

Fill in the remaining six months so that there is a full year cash flow budget. Then answer these questions:

ACME WIDGET COMPANY
Cash Flow Budget for Year Three

	Jan.	Feb.	Mar.	Apr.	May	June
Sales of regular widgets	13,750	13,750	13,750	13,750	13,750	13,750
Sales of fluted widgets	—	—	—	—	1,380	1,840
Total sales	13,750	13,750	13,750	13,750	15,130	15,590
Collections from previous year	11,400	11,400	5,700	—	—	—
Collections from current year	—	—	13,750	13,750	13,750	13,750
Total collections	11,400	11,400	19,450	13,750	13,750	13,750
Inventory payments, previous year	12,500	—	—	—	—	—
Inventory payments, regular	—	6,875	6,875	6,875	6,875	6,875
Inventory payments, fluted						660
Total inventory payments	12,500	6,875	6,875	6,875	6,875	7,535
Office expenses and interest payments	200	200	200	200	200	200
Advertising	—	750	—	1,000	750	—
Salaries and Christmas bonus	2,700	2,700	2,700	3,450	3,450	3,450
Payment of taxes	—	—	—	9,150	—	—
Payment for fluted widget machine	—	—	18,000	—	—	—
Payment of dividends	—	—	—	—	—	—
TOTAL CASH PAID OUT	15,400	10,525	27,775	20,675	11,275	11,185
TOTAL CASH IN	11,400	11,400	19,450	13,750	13,750	13,750
NET CASH FLOW	(4,000)	875	(8,325)	(6,925)	2,475	2,565
Cash on hand, beginning	8,710	4,710	5,585	(2,740)	(9,665)	(7,190)
Cash on hand, ending	4,710	5,585	(2,740)	(9,665)	(7,190)	(4,625)
Additional cash needed			2,740	6,925		

1. Suppose Acme can borrow $12,000 for six months at 9 percent annual interest rate. Will Acme be able to pay

off the loan and the interest? Or will a longer loan need to be made?

2. Should Acme put off the purchase of the fluted widget machine until later? If so, when? Or should Acme borrow on a long-term basis in order to purchase the machine? It is possible that a five-year loan at 10 percent annual interest can be obtained to pay for the machine. Interest charges over the period of the loan will be $5,400. Is this the way Acme should go?

3. Can Acme afford to pay dividends? Can it afford to pay the Christmas bonus? Will it need to borrow additional money to make these payments?

You can probably think of other pertinent questions that the Acme managers must face. Working out the answers to these questions will help you appreciate the value of a cash flow budget.

SUMMARY

The cash flow is an extremely valuable management tool. It pinpoints the flow of cash into and out of the company. It spotlights potential cash flow problems. It helps to determine the best ways of obtaining cash when it is going to be needed.

The cash flow budget can have various formats. We have used a common one, but not the only possible one. The specific needs of the business and the specific circumstances will determine the format that will focus on the information needed.

The cash flow budget can have various formats. We have used a common one, but not the only possible one. The specific needs of the business and the specific circumstances will determine the format that will focus on the information needed.

Effective and profitable management is much more likely if attention is paid to a cash flow budget. The balance sheet and the income statement cannot be as helpful in forcing the kind of planning that will avoid the embarrassment of running out of cash. We said earlier that a company can be doing well in sales and profits and still go broke. A cash flow budget can prevent this unfortunate occurrence.

The following diagram charts the flow of cash into, through, and out of the business. A study of this diagram can help you to improve your understanding of cash flow.

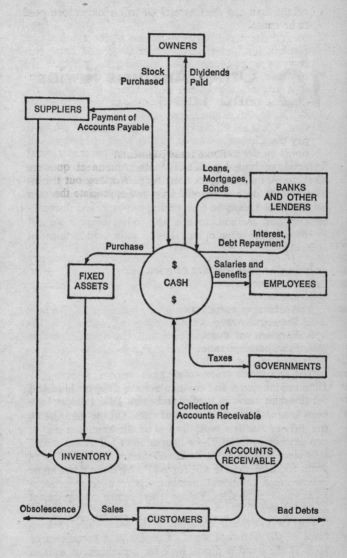

10. Other Analysis Ratios and Tools

IN PREVIOUS CHAPTERS we covered several financial analysis ratios and tools. Among them were working capital, average collection period, inventory turnover, return on equity, return on invested capital, return on assets used, cash-on-cash return, payback, and discounted cash flow method. In this next-to-last chapter we will briefly consider some other ratios or tools used in financial analysis.

1. Profit as a percentage of sales.
2. Breakeven point.
3. Current ratio.
4. Acid test or quick ratio.
5. Debt-equity ratio.
6. Earnings per share.
7. Price-earnings ratio.

PROFIT AS A PERCENTAGE OF SALES

Different industries and companies have different historical relationships between profits and sales. IBM's profits have been around 12 to 15 percent of sales. On the other hand, the grocery business typically has profits averaging one or two percent of sales. These figures don't tell us too much. It is clear that an extra dollar of sales will produce more profit for IBM than it will for A&P. What we don't know is how much additional investment is required to produce an extra dollar of sales. This is where return on investment analysis helps.

For an individual company it is worthwhile to keep track of the historical trend of profits as a percentage of sales. If the trend is down, look for a problem. A shift in the relationship between profits and sales indicates a need for further analysis. By itself, profit as a percentage of sales is not very important.

BREAKEVEN

Breakeven is a very useful concept and tool. Breakeven is that amount of sales where a company will have neither a profit nor a loss. One more unit or dollar of sales and the company will make a profit. One less unit or dollar of sales and the company will suffer a loss.

Let's compute the Acme Widget breakeven point. First, we will add up all of the costs that will not change, no matter how many widgets we sell. These are called fixed costs. (See Glossary.) While no costs are fixed forever, in the short-run a number of costs are relatively fixed. In the case of Acme (year two), the fixed costs would include the following:

Building occupancy costs (rent or depreciation)	$2,100
Depreciation on machinery and furniture	1,300
Interest paid on borrowed money	900
Office expenses	600
Advertising	3,000
Administrative salaries	24,000
Write-down of obsolete inventory	1,000
Inventory damage	200
	$33,100

Theoretically, these costs would continue, whether or not we sold any widgets. We assume that the advertising outlays, for example, would be spent in anticipation of sales. Salaries paid to the owner-managers would go on. And so forth.

Now we need to consider the costs that will vary with the number of widgets sold. These are called variable costs.

Variable costs will certainly include the cost of sales. We only incur a cost of sales when a sale is made. In our Acme Widget financial reports we have only considered the cost of the raw materials—$1.00 per widget—as a cost of sales.

Is the widget machine operator's salary fixed or variable? We will treat it as variable. If demand was low we would lay off the operator. If demand picked up we would hire another operator for a second shift. The machine operator's salary results in a variable cost of eleven cents per widget.

We will consider the reserve for bad debts as a variable cost. If sales go up, we will need to have a larger reserve. The reserve for bad debts is one percent of sales or two cents for each widget sold.

For each widget sold at $2.00, we have variable costs of $1.13. This means that we have 87 cents available from the sale of each widget to pay for fixed costs. How many widgets do we have to sell to exactly cover the fixed costs of $33,100?

$$\$33,100 \div \$0.87 = 38,045.98 \text{ widgets.}$$

In other words, we must sell 38,046 widgets, on which we make 87 cents each, in order to just cover the fixed costs of $33,100.

How much profit do we make when we sell the next widget?

What is the Acme loss if one widget less is sold?

We can show the relationship between sales and profits in a breakeven graph.

The breakeven point on the graph is where the sales line crosses the fixed-cost line. You can estimate from the graph what profits would be generated by selling, say, 60,000 widgets. The profits would be the number of dollars the line is above the fixed cost level at 60,000 units. See the dotted line that traces up from 60,000 units sold, crosses the fixed-cost line, and then goes across to the dollars line. The profit on sales of 60,000 units is $19,000.

The formula for computing the breakeven point can be stated in this way:

Breakeven units
Fixed Cost ÷
    (Unit Selling Price — Variable Cost per Unit)

Breakeven analysis often looks at the number of units required to break even and asks whether or not the company can reasonably expect to sell that many units. If the projection of breakeven point comes up with a number of units that is far too many to expect to sell, then there is a problem. Perhaps fixed costs are too high and must be cut. Perhaps the variable costs are out of line. Perhaps a different kind of selling effort is needed in order to sell more

Breakeven Graph

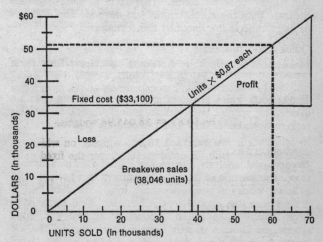

units. Or perhaps the project should be abandoned before it produces a big loss.

Breakeven analysis is one of the most valuable planning tools. Good managers find themselves using it often.

CURRENT RATIO

The current ratio equals current assets divided by current liabilities. Bankers and other lenders look at the current ratio as a measure of a company's ability to pay its debts.

Lenders like to see a current ratio of 2 to 1 or more. In other words, current assets should be twice as large as current liabilities.

The idea of the current ratio is that if current assets were all turned into cash upon liquidation of the business, current liabilities would have to be paid off. Then how much would be left over to pay off long-term liabilities? A 2 to 1 current ratio indicates that current liabilities could be paid off and an equal amount would still be left to pay other debts.

ACID TEST OR QUICK RATIO

The acid test or quick ratio was developed because lenders realized that all of the current assets might not actually be

worth what is shown on the balance sheet. Accounts receivable might not all be collectible. Inventory might contain many obsolete items. Therefore a more rigorous
measure than the current ratio was devised. The acid test
or quick ratio is calculated by this formula:

$$\text{Quick Ratio} = \frac{\text{Cash} + \text{Marketable Securities} + \text{Accounts and Notes Receivable}}{\text{Current Liabilities}}$$

Those assets which are most easily converted into cash are
divided by current liabilities to give the quick ratio. This
ratio must be better than 1 to 1 to pass the acid test.

DEBT-EQUITY RATIO

Lenders and analysts like to see that the owners have a
reasonable portion of the total investment in a business.

Some kinds of businesses have long-term debt that is
greater than the capital in the business. Real estate ventures usually have small amounts of capital and large
mortgages. Utilities usually have a larger portion of their
invested capital from debt and a smaller portion from
equity. But many other kinds of businesses have a majority of the company investment in the form of capital.

The debt-equity ratio equals debt divided by equity.

$$\text{Debt-Equity Ratio} = \frac{\text{Long-Term Liabilities}}{\text{Capital}}$$

EARNINGS PER SHARE

Earnings per share are calculated by this formula:

$$\text{Earnings Per Share} = \frac{\text{Net Profit After Taxes}}{\text{Outstanding Shares of Stock}}$$

This measure is used by stock market analysts and investors. They are particularly interested in growth in earnings
per share. This is thought to be an important measure of
company performance.

As we have seen, the calculation of net profit after taxes
is not exact. Many factors can affect the profits. We have
also seen their profits are not cash and are not available for
payment to owners of the company's stock. Numbers
showing earnings per share must be approached with caution.

PRICE-EARNINGS RATIO

The price-earnings ratio (p/e ratio) relates the earnings per share to the price per share of stock. The formula for computing the p/e ratio is:

$$p/e \text{ ratio} = \frac{\text{Price per share}}{\text{Earnings per share}}$$

The price per share is the market price on the stock market, or the price in an acquisition or some other transaction. Earnings per share can be those for the last accounting period (fiscal or calendar year) or those projected for the next one.

In the go-go days of speculation on the stock market in the 1960's, any stock with "computer" in its name might have a p/e ratio of 100 or 200 or more. In other words, a stock with earnings per share of $1.00 would be selling on the stock market for $100, $200, or more per share.

In the bust that followed, these same stocks plummeted. Their p/e ratios went down to 3 or 4 or 5. With the same $1.00 earnings per share the stock could be purchased for $3 or $4 or $5. What was the stock really worth?

Who knows? A more normal range for well-established companies in more normal times is a p/e ratio of from 6 to 12.

What is a reasonable p/e ratio? It depends. If you are buying control of a company, you are buying the ability to control the disposition of its assets and future earnings. Control is obviously of value. The worth of control can be analyzed by various methods—discounted cash flow, payback, cash-on-cash return, and so forth. A company might be worth nothing or a thousand times its stated earnings. A premium is usually paid to obtain control.

The situation is quite different if you are buying a tiny fraction of the company's stock—as you normally do when you buy a publicly-traded stock on the market. Then the p/e ratio depends on what the "market" believes. If all the potential and actual buyers of the stock think the company will grow rapidly and make ever-increasing earnings, then there will be a high p/e ratio. If people think the company is faltering, then the p/e ratio will be low. The p/e ratio is derived from the expectations of the future held by potential and actual buyers in the market.

Experience indicates that a large number of people turn out to be wrong in their expectations. Stocks are seldom worth as little as people think they are in recession times.

If you want to gamble in the stock market, other books can help you. The price-earnings ratio is not much of a tool of financial analysis.

Of the various analysis ratios and tools discussed in this chapter, breakeven point is the most useful to the business manager.

11. What You Have Learned—A Summary

IN MY BUSINESS LIFE I have followed a number of precepts. Two apply here.

I believe in repetition. Presenting ideas several times in different contexts helps build understanding. (Just as repeating sales messages can help build sales.) So I am going to repeat the main ideas presented in this book once again.

I also believe in the preacher's approach—tell 'em what you're going to tell 'em . . . then tell 'em . . . then tell 'em what you told 'em. Now it is time to tell you what I told you.

Let's review what you have learned if you have come this far.

Accounting is a method of keeping score in business. It uses dollars as the basic score, just as points are the score in football, goals are the score in hockey, and runs are the score in baseball.

The methods of keeping score with dollars is what accounting is all about. Certain basic financial reports are used to present the score—the balance sheet, income statement, statement of retained earnings, and statement of changes in financial position. A variety of ratios, percentages, and other tools or equations are used to analyze the scores—as sports enthusiasts use earned run averages, goals against, point spreads, and so forth.

The scores on financial reports do not represent real spendable dollars available. A major reason for this is that businesses use the accrual method of accounting. Individuals keep track of cash receipts or payments. Businesses keep track of transactions that create assets or liabilities. These transactions accrue to the company or accrue to the company's debtors or owners. The transactions do not

131

necessarily represent the transfer of actual cash money at the time the transactions occur. Thus the financial reports of a business show transactions or accruals. They do not usually show the actual flow of real, spendable, cash money.

Financial reports are not exact. Many of the items are estimated. The estimates reflect the hopes, fears, perspectives, and judgments of human beings. Different people see things differently. Estimates differ. So financial reports for the same company for the same period will differ, depending on who decides on the uncertain items.

Financial reports are made for different purposes. Reports for the tax authorities usually seek to minimize the profits on which taxes must be paid. The same reports prepared for would-be investors may seek to maximize profits.

There is no such thing as the one and only, completely accurate financial report. If you know who prepared the financial report, and for what purpose it was prepared, you will have a much better idea of what the real score is.

THE BALANCE SHEET

The balance sheet shows the financial position of a company frozen at one specific point in time.

The balance sheet balances. On the left side (or the top) are listed assets (things of value owned by the company).

On the right side (or the lower portion) are listed liabilities (debts the company owes). Below liabilities are listed capital (the owners' share).

$$\text{Assets} = \text{Liabilities} + \text{Capital}$$

Every entry into or out of the balance sheet must be balanced by a corresponding entry in another part of the balance sheet.

The principal assets shown on the balance sheet are:
Cash
Marketable Securities
Accounts Receivable (amounts owed to the company by its customers)
Reserves for Doubtful Accounts or *Allowances for Bad*

Debts (a reduction in accounts receivable to provide for accounts that may not be paid)

Inventory (stock to be sold to customers, often divided into raw materials, work in process, and finished goods)

Reserve for Obsolescence (a reduction in the value of the inventory to allow for possible unsalable goods)

Prepaid Expenses (amounts paid for goods or services that will come to the company in the future)

Fixed Assets (machinery, land, buildings, improvements to rented property, and other assets used to create inventory or generate sales)

Depreciation (a reduction in the value of fixed assets to account for use and to turn an expenditure into an expense)

Other Assets (copyrights, patents, franchises, licenses, and other intangible items, as well as goodwill)

The principal liabilities are:

Notes Payable (amounts owed to banks or other lenders, due within a year or less)

Accounts Payable (amounts owed to suppliers of goods or services)

Accruals (salaries and other fringe benefits owed to employees but not yet paid, also taxes owed—although sometimes taxes owed are a separate entry)

Long-Term Liabilities (bonds, long-term loans, mortgages not due for more than a year)

The principal items of capital are:

Capital Stock (preferred and common stock issued and sold to investors who become owners)

Retained Earnings (the accumulated after-tax profits of a company less any dividends paid; not available cash)

Assets are listed in the order in which they can be converted to cash. Liabilities are listed in the order in which they are due for payment. Current assets are those likely to become cash within one year. Current liabilities are those debts due within one year.

Working capital equals current assets minus current liabilities. Working capital represents the funds available in a business which circulate to produce profits. As the business operates, the funds in working capital flow from inventory to accounts receivable to cash to accounts payable to inventory.

Current assets divided by current liabilities equals the current ratio. Lenders like to see a current ratio of at least 2 to 1. This gives an indication of a company's ability to pay off its loans.

All items are entered onto the balance sheet at their original cost. Adjustments are made to reduce value, but increases in value are not recognized on financial reports.

Reductions in value come from three principal sources.

Reserves for Doubtful Accounts or Allowances for Bad Debts are reductions in accounts receivable caused by the inability or unwillingness of customers to pay their bills.

Inventory Obsolescence or Reserves for Obsolescence are reductions in the value of inventory. The likely cause of obsolescence is items in the inventory that are going out of style or being shoved aside by more competitive products.

Depreciation or Amortization is the reduction in value of fixed assets or other assets over a period of time. The amount of time is related to useful life and IRS regulations. A machine with a useful life of ten years will have its value reduced to zero (or scrap value) over a period of ten years. The purchase of the machine is an expenditure. The depreciation of the machine is an expense over a ten-year period. Depreciation is a major item that affects the relations of actual cash to financial scores.

The reserve for doubtful accounts is an estimate. It may be wrong. With companies in trouble, the reserve is often understated. Inventory obsolescence is also an estimate. Companies in trouble seldom recognize the true extent of obsolescence. Depreciation is also an estimate. A machine, building, or other fixed asset may have a much shorter or much longer useful life than anticipated. If the fixed asset is only good for producing unsalable goods, then it has no value, no matter how new it is. On the other hand, many companies have assets that keep on generating profits long after they have been depreciated to zero. Some assets, such as buildings, may grow in value with inflation or changes in market conditions. The increase in real value can go on at the same time depreciation is reducing book value.

When looking at a balance sheet, determine whether any assets are valued at more than their true worth. Determine what assets may be valued at less than their true worth.

Then ask what valuable assets are not shown at all on the balance sheet. Most companies do not show many key assets on the balance sheet—computer programs, special production processes, market position, and especially, the knowledge, experience, and capability of the employees who make the company go.

The net worth or book value of a company equals assets minus liabilities (as shown on the balance sheet). But this computation of net worth or book value or owners' equity is not necessarily what the owners would sell the company for. It is not necessarily what a buyer would pay to acquire the company.

The balance sheet and other financial reports are based on certain assumptions:

1. The company is a going concern that will continue in business.
2. The estimates used in the report are essentially correct.
3. The perspective of the report reader is the same as the perspective of the report preparer.
4. All entries are entered at original cost.

If these assumptions are not justified, the balance sheet can be very misleading.

A cautionary note. A company can have so much money tied up in assets that it is unable to pay its bills, even when sales are terrific and profits look good. If customers pay slowly, if too much money is tied up in inventory that doesn't sell quickly, or if the money put into fixed assets is too great, a company can be flat broke when its managers think it is doing well.

The balance sheet is often ignored by people who want to see the "bottom line." I hope that I have been able to convince you of the importance of balance sheet analysis.

THE INCOME STATEMENT
The income statement summarizes the results of a company's operations over a period of time. The "bottom line"—net profit after taxes—appears on the income statement.

The income statement usually follows this format:

Item	Arithmetic
Sales	*minus*
Cost of Sales	*equals*
Gross Profit	*minus*
Operating Expenses	*equals*
Operating Profit	*plus*
Non-operating Income	*minus*
Non-operating Expenses	*equals*
Net Profit Before Taxes	*minus*
Income Taxes	*equals*
Net Profit After Taxes	

Sales are the delivery of goods or services to customers who agree to pay for them. The customers may or may not actually pay. They often will not pay during the period covered by the income statement.

Cost of sales (cost of goods sold) includes the main identifiable costs of the goods sold to the customers. (When only services are sold, usually no cost of sales or gross profit is shown on the income statement.) The costs in cost of sales are the costs associated with goods sold. Goods produced or acquired, but not sold during the period, do not result in a cost of sales. They result in a cost of sales only in the period when they are sold. Until then they sit in inventory.

Cost of sales, purchases, and inventory are related in a simple equation.

Beginning Inventory + Purchases − Ending Inventory =
Cost of Sales

This formula is useful in projecting purchase requirements, ending inventory, and cost of sales.

Gross profit equals sales minus cost of sales.

Operating expenses include the expenses incurred to generate sales, fulfill orders, collect from customers, keep the accounts, and so forth. Many of these expenses are cash expenditures during the period, But some are expenditures that have occurred or will occur in other periods.

Depreciation, amortization, additions to reserves, write-downs, and write-offs of obsolete inventory, bad debts, or worthless assets of other kinds are also expenses. These expenses do not require the expenditure of cash during the period.

Non-operating income is income that arises from sources that are not part of the regular operations of the business. Non-operating expense is most often interest paid to borrow money.

Income taxes are the taxes owed to various government taxing bodies on the net profit before taxes for the period.

Net profit after taxes is the final result of all the subtractions and additions on the income statement. Net profit after taxes is not spendable cash. Actual cash generated by operations may be much more or much less.

The statement of retained earnings or reconciliation of retained earnings shows how the retained earnings on the balance sheet have changed as a result of activities during the period. The statement shows:

> Beginning Retained Earnings   *plus*
> Net Profit After Taxes   *minus*
> Dividends Paid   *equals*
> Ending Retained Earnings.

Remember, retained earnings aren't spendable cash either.

The income statement is usually the main format used for budgeting. It is important, but keep in mind that various transactions of importance affect the balance sheet but not the income statement.

STATEMENT OF CHANGES IN FINANCIAL POSITION

This statement shows how funds flowed into, through, and out of the company during the period. It focuses on working capital as the reservoir of funds. The statement follows this format:

> Sources of Working Capital
>> Net Profit After Taxes
>> Depreciation and Non-Cash Expenses
>>> Total From Operations
>> Sale of Fixed Assets or Other Non-Current Assets
>> Stock Issued
>> Long-Term Borrowing
>>> Total Sources of Working Capital

Uses of Working Capital
    Purchase of Fixed Assets or Other Non-Current
      Assets
    Payments of Dividends
    Reduction of Long-Term Debt
    Purchase of Stock
      Total Uses of Working Capital
Net Change in Working Capital

Analysis of Changes in Working Capital Items

The statement of changes in financial position is derived
from the balance sheet and income statement. It makes
clearer the flow of funds that brought about changes in the
balance sheet.

CASH FLOW BUDGET

The cash flow statement or budget is normally not shown.
It does not appear in public financial reports. But it is an
extremely valuable management planning tool. It pinpoints
the flow of cash into and out of the business. It spotlights
cash flow problems and allows managers to avoid embarrassment, not to mention bankruptcy. Various formats can
be used. A monthly chart showing cash in and out is often
the most helpful.

ANALYZING FINANCIAL REPORTS

Comparative reports make it easier to analyze. There are
several types of comparisons.

Comparison with the past shows current figures alongside figures from the past. What past? This depends on the
needs. It may be the immediately preceding period. If the
report is for a period shorter than a year, it may be compared with the similar period in the previous year. Or the
comparison may be with an average of past periods.

Comparing actual figures with budgeted or planned figures is especially valuable. For managers, there is no substitute for comparing what actually happened with what
you planned or expected to happen. Significant variances
from the plan or budget should be carefully studied to determine what changes are necessary.

Showing each item as a percentage of sales helps in
analysis. If operating expenses were 52 percent of sales

this year and 60 percent of sales last year, this is much more meaningful than knowing that operating expenses were $1,387,000 this year and $1,386,000 last year.

Dollar changes from one period to the next are often shown. Even more useful are percentage changes. It helps to see that sales went up 12 percent while operating profit increased by 18 percent.

When percentages are not given on financial reports, it helps to compute them before sitting down to make an analysis.

$$\text{Average Collection Period} = \frac{\text{Average Accounts Receivable}}{\text{Annual Sales}} \times 365$$

Average collection period is the number of days required, on the average, to collect amounts owed to the company by its customers. Changes in average collection period can signal developing problems that may lead to serious cash shortages.

$$\text{Inventory Turnover} = \frac{\text{Cost of Sales}}{\text{Average Inventory}}$$

Inventory turnover tells how many times (theoretically) the inventory of a company is replenished during the year. The faster inventory turns over, the less investment is required to operate the business. Changes in inventory turnover can signal problems with inventory obsolescence or sales efforts. High inventory turnover does not necessarily mean that all items in inventory are selling satisfactorily. Remember the 80–20 rule. Concentration of sales may mean that a few items are selling very quickly while many others just lie there.

Return on investment (ROI) is the best overall method of analyzing a company's (or division's) financial performance. Return on investment indicates how well the business is using its resources to produce profits. There are several principal methods of computing return on investment.

1. $\text{Return on Equity} = \dfrac{\text{Net Profit After Taxes}}{\text{Owner's Equity}}$

ROE is a good method of analyzing whether or not the owner's investment is being effectively used to produce profits.

2. Return on Invested Capital =

$$\frac{\text{Net Profit After Taxes} + \text{Interest on Long-Term Debt}}{\text{Capital} + \text{Long-Term Debt}}$$

ROIC is particularly useful in analyzing companies that have a significant amount of long-term debt. It looks at the total investment rather than at only a portion of it.

3. Return on Assets Used =

$$\frac{\text{Operating Profit}}{\text{Assets Used to Generate Operating Profit}}$$

ROAU is used to analyze divisions or departments of companies, where the headquarters has control of liabilities and capital.

All ROI formulas produce percentages. These percentages can be compared with industry ROI percentages, with the company's historical ROI percentages, with budgeted ROI percentages, or with ROI percentages likely from other uses of investment funds. These comparisons of ROI percentages are much more meaningful than a bare percentage by itself.

Other measures are used to analyze potential opportunities.

$$\text{Cash-on-Cash Return} = \frac{\text{Cash Taken Out}}{\text{Cash Put In}}$$

Cash-on-cash return is most often used in real estate or similar operations where little or no cash is kept in the business. Cash-on-cash return gets around the effects of depreciation and other non-cash items that affect other ROI formulas.

Payback period is an offshoot of cash analysis. It looks at opportunities and asks, "How long will it take to pay back this investment? How soon can we get our money back?"

A dollar in hand today is worth more than a dollar that becomes available in the future. In business, investments are always being made today to produce returns in the future. The returns from these investments are often uneven. A method has been developed to analyze these investments. This method is called the discounted cash flow or present value method.

The discounted cash flow or present value method brings all investments, expenditures, and returns to their current, today, value. It discounts future expenditures and earnings to present value. A sophisticated electronic calculator or the table found in the back of this book (and in many other books) is needed to calculate present values.

Present values depend upon three assumptions:

1. The investments, expenditures, and return that can be expected in the future. Usually these can only be estimated.
2. The length of time over which the deal will be analyzed. A deal that looks great over a forty-year span may look awful over a three-year span.
3. The rate of interest that will be used to compute present value. This is the interest rate that can be earned with alternate investments or the rate of return the company expects for its investments.

When these assumptions are made, present values can be calculated and judgments can be made. The discounted cash flow or present value method is a sophisticated and valuable tool of analysis. But it is only as good as the assumptions that underlie the calculations.

Profit as a percentage of sales is a frequently reported number. It has a rough-and-ready usefulness in indicating trends and performance. But industries and companies vary greatly. Return on investment is a much more significant figure.

Breakeven point is that amount of sales that will just cover fixed and variable costs. More sales will produce a profit. Less sales will produce a loss. Breakeven is usually stated in terms of number of units or dollars that must be sold. It is a valuable management planning tool.

Lenders like to look at the current ratio. More conservative lenders apply the acid test or compute the quick ratio. This is a more rigorous measure of a company's ability to pay its debts.

$$\text{Acid Test Ratio} = \frac{\text{Cash + Marketable Securities + Accounts Receivable}}{\text{Current Liabilities}}$$

In analyzing publicly-traded stocks, earnings per share, book value per share, and the price-earnings ratio are often used. These are not analysis tools that are much help in managing a company. Stockholders, security analysts and some managers think these numbers are more important than they really are.

FINALLY

In this book I have tried to cover the financial terms, concepts, formulas, equations, reports, comparisons, and ideas that I have found useful in 25 years of business life.

This is certainly not all there is to know about financial reports and their analysis. But it is enough. It is all that needs to be covered in this book. The libraries and bookstores are packed with much longer books that cover these topics—and many other topics in accounting—in much greater, even exhaustive, detail. You should have no trouble in getting help from these books when you need it.

If you have gotten this far, you should suffer no embarrassment in talking with accountants. Ask them when you need help. After all, they are the professionals. They ought to know more than you do about accounting. But you must know enough to ask the right questions and to understand and interpret the answers you get. You should now know enough to do this.

Whenever you feel shaky, run through the Glossary quickly. Go over the summary again. Go over the summary section of each chapter. Look in the Index for the pages on which you can get a review of a specific item. This kind of quick refresher can shore you up when you need help. This book has been a study tool. Now it should be a reference guide.

Let me close with two last thoughts.

1. Remember that financial reports are not exact and the numbers are not real cash. Financial reports are scorecards—made up of estimates, structured in terms of a specific perspective, and designed for purposes that may differ from yours. Financial reports are primarily means of presenting scores in business. Do not be fooled into believing they tell the full truth. Don't take financial reports for more than they really are.
2. Remember that financial reports are not the only measure of what is valuable. The worth of human

beings is not shown in financial reports. Love and truth and beauty and adventure and justice and many, many more of life's most important things cannot be pinned down by the numbers on financial reports.

Never, ever let your life be dominated by the numbers on financial reports. Use them as tools—to help you achieve important and worthwhile goals. Financial reports are totally unsuitable tools for many of life's most important goals.

When you are on your deathbed, you won't want to summarize your life by saying you had the best ROI, the soundest balance sheet, or the largest net profit after taxes. Keep your mind on those things that you will want to look back on with pride as your life draws to a close. I don't think that financial reports or accounting results will be among those things.

Appendix

ACME WIDGET—YEAR ONE—
BALANCE SHEET WORKSHEET

1. $20,000 stock sale: + $20,000 cash / + $20,000 common stock.

2. Borrow $15,000: + $15,000 cash / + $15,000 notes payable.

3. Purchase machine: + $12,000 fixed assets / + $12,000 accounts payable.

4. Purchase raw materials: + $5,000 inventory—raw materials / + $5,000 accounts payable.

5. Pay rent advance: − $250 cash / + $250 prepaid expenses.

6. Repay bank loan: − $15,000 cash / − $15,000 notes payable.

7. Pay for machine: − $12,000 cash / − $12,000 accounts payable.

8. Pay for raw materials: − $5,000 cash / − $5,000 accounts payable.

9. Purchase $40,000 raw materials: + $40,000 inventory—raw materials / + $40,000 accounts payable.

   Pay for $30,000: − $30,000 cash / − $30,000 accounts payable.

10. Manufacture 41,000 widgets: + $41,000 inventory—finished goods / − $41,000 inventory—raw materials.

11. 36,500 widgets sold: — $36,500 inventory—finished goods / — $36,500 retained earnings.

    Sell $73,000 worth of widgets: + $73,000 accounts receivable / + $73,000 retained earnings.

    Customers pay $56,000: + $56,000 cash / — $56,000 accounts receivable.

12. Depreciate machine: — $1,200 depreciation of fixed assets / — $1,200 retained earnings.

13. 11 months' rent and one month's advance paid at $250 per month: — $3,000 cash / — $2,750 retained earnings / + $250 prepaid expenses.

14. First month's prepaid rent used: — $250 prepaid expenses / — $250 retained earnings.

15. Salaries at $2,000 per month, last month owed: — $22,000 cash / + $2,000 accrual / — $24,000 retained earnings.

16. Office expenses of $50 a month: — $600 cash / — $600 retained earnings.

17. $2,500 advertising: — $2,500 cash / — $2,500 retained earnings.

18. Income taxes due of $1,150: + $1,150 accruals / — $1,150 retained earnings.

ACME WIDGET—YEAR ONE—TRIAL BALANCE WORKSHEET

ASSETS

Cash	Accounts Receivable	Inventory Raw Materials	Inventory Finished Goods
+20,000	+73,000	+ 5,000	+41,000
+15,000	−56,000	+40,000	−36,500
− 250	+17,000	−41,000	+ 4,500
−15,000		+ 4,000	
−12,000			
− 5,000			
−30,000			
+56,000			
− 3,000			
−22,000			
− 600			
− 2,500			
+ 650			

Prepaid Expenses	Fixed Assets	Depreciation
+250	+12,000	− 1,200
+250		
−250		
+250		

TOTAL
ASSETS
37,200

LIABILITIES

Accounts Payable	Notes Payable	Accruals
+12,000	+15,000	+2,000
+ 5,000	—15,000	+1,150
—12,000		
— 5,000	—0—	+3,150
+40,000		
—30,000		
+10,000		

TOTAL
LIABILITIES
13,150

CAPITAL

Common Stock	Retained Earnings
+20,000	+73,000
	—36,500
	— 1,200
	— 2,750
	— 250
	—24,000
	— 600
	— 2,500
	— 1,150
	+ 4,050

TOTAL
CAPITAL
24,050

ACME WIDGET COMPANY
BALANCE SHEET
First Year of Operations

ASSETS			LIABILITIES AND CAPITAL	
			LIABILITIES	
Cash		$ 650	Accounts Payable	$10,000
Accounts Receivable		17,000	Notes Payable	—0—
Inventory			Accruals	3,150
Raw Materials	4,000		Total Liabilities	$13,150
Finished Goods	4,500			
Total		8,500		
Prepaid Expenses		250		
Fixed Assets	12,000		**CAPITAL**	
Less			Common Stock	$20,000
Depreciation	1,200		Retained Earnings	4,050
Net Fixed Assets		10,800	Total Capital	$24,050
			Total Liabilities	
Total Assets		$37,200	and Capital	$37,200

ACME WIDGET—YEAR TWO—
BALANCE SHEET WORKSHEET

1. Sell 75,000 widgets: — $75,000 inventory—finished goods / — $75,000 retained earnings.

   $150,000 sales: + $150,000 accounts receivable / + $150,000 retained earnings.

2. Collect $17,000 and $120,000: + $137,000 cash / — $137,000 accounts receivable.

   Set up reserve for doubtful accounts: — $1,500 reserve for doubtful accounts / — $1,500 retained earnings.

3. Buy $87,500 raw materials: + $87,500 inventory—raw materials / $87,500 accounts payable.

   Pay $10,000 plus $75,000 to raw material supplier: — $85,000 cash / — $85,000 accounts payable.

4. Pay widget machine operator $8,400: — $7,700 cash / + $700 accruals / — $8,400 retained earnings.

   Pay off final month's salary for year one to owner-managers: — $2,000 cash / — $2,000 accruals.

   Pay salary for year two to owner-managers: — $22,000 cash / + $2,000 accruals / — $24,000 retained earnings.

5. Make 76,500 widgets: — $76,500 inventory—raw materials / + $76,500 inventory—finished goods.

6. Purchase $840 of furniture: — $840 cash / + $840 fixed assets.

   Depreciate at $10 per month for 10 months: — $100 depreciation / — $100 retained earnings.

7. Inventory damage of $200: — $200 inventory—raw materials / — $200 retained earnings.

   Write down 1,000 widgets: — $1,000 inventory—finished goods / — $1,000 retained earnings.

8. Acme owners buy more stock: + $10,000 cash / + $10,000 common stock.

Acme owners pay $10,000 down on building: — $10,000 cash / + $10,000 fixed assets.

Acme owners give $20,000 mortgage on building: + $20,000 fixed assets / + $20,000 long-term liabilities.

Interest paid at 9% on $20,000 is paid for six months: — $900 cash / — $900 retained earnings.

Depreciate building for 6 months at $100 per month: — $600 depreciation / — $600 retained earnings.

Rent paid for 5 months at $250 per month: — $1,250 cash / — $1,250 retained earnings.

Prepaid rent used up: — $250 prepaid expenses / — $250 retained earnings.

 9. Office expenses of $600: — $600 cash / — $600 retained earnings.

Advertising of $3,000: — $3,000 cash / — $3,000 retained earnings.

10. Purchase license: — $1,500 cash / + $1,500 intangible assets.

11. Pay dividend: — $3,000 cash / — $3,000 retained earnings.

12. Acme buys CD: — $1,000 cash / + $1,000 marketable securities.

13. Depreciate widget machine: — $1,200 depreciation / — $1,200 retained earnings.

14. Pay off previous year's taxes: — $1,150 cash / — $1,150 accruals.

15. Owe $9,150 in income taxes on current year operations: + $9,150 accruals / — $9,150 retained earnings.

ACME WIDGET—YEAR TWO—TRIAL BALANCE WORKSHEET

ASSETS

Cash	Marketable Securities	Accounts Receivable	Reserve for Doubtful Accounts
+ 650	—	+ 17,000	—
+137,000	+1,000	+150,000	−1,500
− 85,000		−137,000	
− 7,700		+ 30,000	
− 2,000			
− 22,000			
+ 10,000			
− 10,000			
− 900			
− 1,250			
− 600			
− 3,000			
− 1,500			
− 840			
− 3,000			
− 1,000			
− 1,150			
+ 7,710			

Inventory Raw Materials	Inventory Finished Goods	Prepaid Expenses
+ 4,000	+ 4,500	+250
+87,500	−75,000	−250
−76,500	+76,500	−0−
− 200	− 1,000	
+14,800	+ 5,000	

Fixed Assets	Depreciation	Intangible Assets
+12,000	−1,200	—
+ 840	− 100	+1,500
+10,000	− 600	
+20,000	−1,200	
+42,840	−3,100	

TOTAL ASSETS
98,250

LIABILITIES

Accounts Payable	Accruals	Long-Term Debt
+10,000	+ 3,150	—
+87,500	+ 700	
−85,000	− 2,000	+20,000
+12,500	+ 2,000	
	− 1,150	
	+ 9,150	
	+11,850	

TOTAL LIABILITIES
44,350

CAPITAL

Common Stock	Retained Earnings
+20,000	+ 4,050
+10,000	+150,000
+30,000	− 75,000
	− 1,500
	− 8,400
	− 24,000
	− 100
	− 200
	− 1,000
	− 900
	− 600
	− 1,250
	− 250
	− 600
	− 3,000
	− 3,000
	− 1,200
	− 9,150
	+ 23,900

TOTAL CAPITAL
53,900

TOTAL LIABILITIES AND CAPITAL
98,250

ACME WIDGET COMPANY
Balance Sheet
Second Year of Operations

ASSETS			LIABILITIES AND CAPITAL		
	Year Two	Year One		Year Two	Year One
CURRENT ASSETS			CURRENT LIABILITIES		
Cash	$ 7,710	$ 650	Accounts Payable	$12,500	$10,000
Marketable Securities	1,000	—	Accruals	11,850	3,150
Accounts Receivable	30,000	17,000			
Less Reserve for Doubtful Accounts	1,500	—	Total Current Liabilities	24,350	13,150
Net Accounts Receivable	28,500	17,000	LONG-TERM LIABILITIES		
Inventory			Long-Term Debt	20,000	—
Raw Materials	14,800	4,000	Total Long-Term Liabilities	20,000	—
Finished Goods	5,000	4,500			
Total Inventory	19,800	8,500	TOTAL LIABILITIES	44,350	13,150
Prepaid Expenses	–0–	250	CAPITAL		
			Common Stock	30,000	20,000
Total Current Assets	57,010	26,400	Retained Earnings	23,900	4,050
NON-CURRENT ASSETS			TOTAL CAPITAL	53,900	24,050
Fixed Assets	42,840	12,000			
Less depreciation	3,100	1,200			
Net Fixed Assets	39,740	10,800			
Intangible Assets	1,500	—			
Total Non-Current Assets	41,240	10,800			
TOTAL ASSETS	$98,250	$37,200	TOTAL LIABILITIES AND CAPITAL	$98,250	$37,200

ACME WIDGET COMPANY
Comparative Income Statement for Year Two

Item	Year Two	Percentage of Sales	Year One	Percentage of Sales
Sales	$150,000	100.0%	$73,000	100.0%
Cost of Sales	76,200	50.8	36,500	50.0
Gross Profit	73,800	49.2	36,500	50.0
Salaries	32,400	21.6	24,000	32.9
Advertising	3,000	2.0	2,500	3.4
Machinery Deprec.	1,200	0.8	1,200	1.6
Furniture & Fixt.	100	0.1	—	—
Building Space Costs	2,100	1.4	3,000	4.1
Other	2,100	1.4	600	0.8
Total Operating Expenses	40,900	27.3	31,300	42.9
Operating Profit	32,900	21.9	5,200	7.1
Non-Operating Income And Expense	900	0.6	—	—
Income Taxes	9,150	6.1	1,150	1.6
Net Profit After Taxes	$ 22,850	15.2%	$ 4,050	5.5%

Acme Fluted Widget Machine Purchase Decision

Assumptions:

1. Profit—

Year	Units Sold	× Price/Unit	= Sales	−	Expenses*	= Profit
1	14,000	$2.30	$ 32,200		$ 32,100	$ 100
2	18,000	2.40	43,200		38,700	4,500
3	20,000	2.40	48,000		42,000	6,000
4	20,000	2.50	50,000		42,000	8,000
	72,000		$173,400		$154,800	$18,600

* Expenses = $1.10 raw materials + $0.55 in variable operating expenses for each unit, plus $9,000 operator's salary.

2. Time—Four years
3. Interest rate—6%

Discounted Cash Flow:

	Cash Paid Out				Cash Received		
Year	Amount	× Present Value Factor	= Present Value		Amount	× Present Value Factor	= Present Value
0	$18,000	1.000	$18,000		$ —	—	—
1	—	—	—		100	.9434	$ 94.34
2	—	—	—		4,500	.8900	4,005.00
3	—	—	—		6,000	.8396	5,037.60
4	—	—	—		8,000	.7921	6,336.80
Total	$18,000		$18,000		$18,600		$15,473.74

ACME WIDGET COMPANY
Statement of Changes in Financial Position
Year Two

Sources of working capital	
Net profit after taxes	$22,850
Depreciation	1,900
Total from operations	24,750
Stock issued	10,000
Long-term borrowing	20,000
Total sources of working capital	54,750
Uses of working capital	
Purchase of fixed assets	30,840
Purchase of intangible asset	1,500
Dividends paid	3,000
Reduction in long-term debt	–0–
Stock purchased	–0–
Total uses of working capital	35,340
Increase in working capital	19,410
Changes in working capital	
Cash and marketable securities	8,060
Accounts receivable, net after reserve	11,500
Inventory, net after write-down	11,300
Prepaid expenses	(250)
Accounts payable	(2,500)
Accruals	(8,700)
	19,410
Working capital at beginning of year	13,250
Working capital at end of year	32,660

Figure 7

ACME WIDGET COMPANY
Cash Flow Budget for Year Three

	Jan.	Feb.	Mar.	Apr.	May	June
Sales of regular widgets	13,750	13,750	13,750	13,750	13,750	13,750
Sales of fluted widgets	—	—	—	—	1,380	1,840
Total sales	13,750	13,750	13,750	13,750	15,130	15,590
Collections from previous year	11,400	11,400	5,700	—	—	—
Collections from current year	—	—	13,750	13,750	13,750	13,750
Total collections	11,400	11,400	19,450	13,750	13,750	13,750
Inventory payments, previous year	12,500	—	—	—	—	—
Inventory payments, regular	—	6,875	6,875	6,875	6,875	6,875
Inventory payments, fluted	—	—	—	—	—	660
Total inventory payments	12,500	6,875	6,875	6,875	6,875	7,535
Office expenses and interest payments	200	200	200	200	200	200
Advertising	—	750	—	1,000	750	—
Salaries and Christmas bonus	2,700	2,700	2,700	3,450	3,450	3,450
Payment of taxes	—	—	—	9,150	—	—
Payment for fluted widget machine	—	—	18,000	—	—	—
Payment of dividends	—	—	—	—	—	—
TOTAL CASH PAID OUT	15,400	10,525	27,775	20,675	11,275	11,185
TOTAL CASH IN	11,400	11,400	19,450	13,750	13,750	13,750
NET CASH FLOW	(4,000)	875	(8,325)	(6,925)	2,475	2,565
Cash on hand, beginning	8,710	4,710	5,585	(2,740)	(9,665)	(7,190)
Cash on hand, ending	4,710	5,585	(2,740)	(9,665)	(7,190)	(4,625)
Additional cash needed			2,740	6,925		

July	Aug.	Sep.	Oct.	Nov.	Dec.	TOTAL	
11,000	11,000	16,500	16,500	13,750	13,750	165,000	
2,300	2,530	3,220	3,450	3,680	3,680	22,080	Year Three Sales (income
13,300	13,530	19,720	19,950	17,430	17,430	187,080	statement)
—	—	—	—	—	—	28,500	Beginning Accounts
15,130	15,590	13,300	13,530	19,720	19,950	152,220	Receivable = 28,500
15,130	15,590	13,300	13,530	19,720	19,950	180,720	Plus Sales = 187,080
							Minus Collections = 180,720
							Equals Ending
							Accounts
							Receivable = 34,860
							(balance
							sheet)
—	—	—	—	—	—	12,500	
6,875	5,500	5,500	8,250	8,250	6,875	75,625	
880	1,100	1,210	1,540	1,650	1,760	8,800	
7,755	6,600	6,710	9,790	9,900	8,635	96,925	(balance sheet)
200	200	200	200	200	200	2,400	(income statement)
—	—	750	—	750	—	4,000	(income statement)
3,450	3,450	3,450	3,450	3,450	5,450	41,150	(income statement)
—	—	—	—	—	—	9,150	(balance sheet)
—	—	—	—	—	—	18,000	(fixed asset—balance sheet)
—	—	—	3,000	—	—	3,000	(balance sheet)
11,405	10,250	11,110	16,440	14,300	14,285	174,625	
15,130	15,590	13,300	13,530	19,720	19,950	180,720	
3,725	5,340	2,190	(2,910)	5,420	5,665	6,095	
(4,625)	(900)	4,440	6,630	3,720	9,140		
(900)	4,440	6,630	3,720	9,140	14,805	14,805	(balance sheet)
						9,665	

PRESENT VALUE TABLE—The Present Value of $1.00

INTEREST RATE

Number of Years	5%	6%	7%	8%	9%	10%	11%	12%
1	.9524	.9434	.9346	.9259	.9174	.9091	.9009	.8929
2	.9070	.8900	.8734	.8573	.8417	.8264	.8116	.7972
3	.8638	.8396	.8163	.7938	.7722	.7513	.7312	.7118
4	.8227	.7921	.7629	.7350	.7084	.6830	.6587	.6355
5	.7835	.7473	.7130	.6806	.6499	.6209	.5935	.5674
6	.7462	.7050	.6663	.6302	.5963	.5645	.5846	.5066
7	.7107	.6651	.6227	.5835	.5470	.5132	.4817	.4523
8	.6768	.6274	.5820	.5403	.5019	.4665	.4339	.4039
9	.6446	.5919	.5439	.5002	.4604	.4241	.3909	.3606
10	.6139	.5584	.5083	.4632	.4224	.3855	.3522	.3220
11	.5847	.5268	.4751	.4289	.3875	.3505	.3173	.2875
12	.5568	.4970	.4440	.3971	.3555	.3186	.2858	.2567
13	.5303	.4688	.4150	.3677	.3262	.2897	.2575	.2292
14	.5051	.4423	.3878	.3405	.2992	.2633	.2320	.2046
15	.4810	.4173	.3624	.3152	.2745	.2394	.2090	.1827
16	.4581	.3936	.3387	.2919	.2519	.2176	.1883	.1631
17	.4363	.3714	.3166	.2703	.2311	.1978	.1696	.1456
18	.4155	.3503	.2959	.2502	.2120	.1799	.1528	.1300
19	.3957	.3305	.2765	.2317	.1945	.1635	.1377	.1161
20	.3769	.3118	.2584	.2145	.1784	.1486	.1241	.1037

The formula for Present Value: $P = \dfrac{1}{(1+I)^n}$

Where P = present value, I = interest rate, and n = number of years.

PRESENT VALUE TABLE—The Present Value of $1.00

INTEREST RATE

Number of Years	13%	14%	15%	16%	17%	18%	19%	20%
1	.8850	.8772	.8696	.8621	.8547	.8475	.8403	.8333
2	.7831	.7695	.7561	.7432	.7305	.7182	.7062	.6944
3	.6931	.6750	.6575	.6407	.6244	.6086	.5934	.5787
4	.6133	.5921	.5718	.5523	.5336	.5158	.4987	.4823
5	.5428	.5194	.4972	.4761	.4561	.4371	.4190	.4019
6	.4803	.4556	.4323	.4104	.3898	.3704	.3521	.3349
7	.4251	.3996	.3759	.3538	.3332	.3139	.2959	.2791
8	.3762	.3506	.3269	.3050	.2848	.2660	.2487	.2326
9	.3329	.3075	.2843	.2630	.2434	.2255	.2090	.1938
10	.2946	.2697	.2472	.2267	.2080	.1911	.1756	.1615
11	.2607	.2366	.2149	.1954	.1778	.1619	.1476	.1346
12	.2307	.2076	.1869	.1685	.1520	.1372	.1240	.1122
13	.2042	.1821	.1625	.1452	.1299	.1163	.1042	.0935
14	.1807	.1597	.1413	.1252	.1110	.0985	.0876	.0779
15	.1599	.1401	.1229	.1079	.0949	.0835	.0736	.0649
16	.1415	.1229	.1069	.0930	.0811	.0708	.0618	.0541
17	.1252	.1078	.0929	.0802	.0693	.0600	.0520	.0451
18	.1108	.0946	.0808	.0691	.0592	.0508	.0437	.0376
19	.0981	.0829	.0703	.0596	.0506	.0431	.0367	.0313
20	.0868	.0728	.0611	.0514	.0433	.0365	.0308	.0261

Index

162

Business Guides from MENTOR and SIGNET